Rhythm Play!

Rhythm Activities and Initiatives
for
Adults, Facilitators, Teachers, and Kids!

Kenya S. Masala

Illustrations by
Crystal Presence & Gabriela Masala

A Juju Studios Publication

Published in conjunction with
FUNdoing
info@fundoing.com

ISBN 0-9746

Kenya Masala and Sourc~
Austin, Texas

kenya@sourceconsultinggroup.com

This book is dedicated to my amazing wife and life partner Gabriela, who brings the magic and music of play to my life every day.

Thanks to Chris Cavert for all the awesome guidance and support, and to Chris, Susana Acosta-Cavert, Debby Short, Maria Skinner, and Gina Fuentes for the phenomenal job of editing!

Photographs: Kenya and Gabriela Masala, Lorie Inman, Robbie Clark, Chris Cavert and Sharon Steehler.

For more information or to purchase additional copies of this book and other materilas, contact Kenya Masala at:
www.sourceconsultinggroup.com
www.rhythmoflifedrumming.com

Terra Ruddy Sola Diamond & River Summer Crystal Yarrow
Baba Olatunji Mamady Keita Fara Tolno Abdoul Doumbia Kulu
Bruce Rudolph Martin Klabunde Jeremy Crytzer Robert Patterson
Arthur Hull Christine Stevens Leza, Kimi, Kep, Sol, Erica, Mike
Thank you!

Contents

*"All people from all walks of life, all colors,
have various things that they can do together to create harmony,
and it is the simplest thing to make music and sing together."*
Baba Olatunji

INTRODUCTION

By reading this book, and experiencing these activities, you'll tap into your innate sense of rhythm; even if you've thought you had none.
Indeed, everyone has rhythm! Having worked with thousands of people all over this country (and folks from other wonderful lands) I can say that everyone has rhythm. It's just a fact. Your heart beats, you walk, you breathe, your eyes blink; it's all rhythm. And, if you didn't have rhythm, you wouldn't know when you were *off* the rhythm! How's that for some fun logic? But really, what it all comes down to is that we all have innate rhythm, and it's a wonderful thing to explore.

Benefits

The benefits of drumming and rhythmic play are many, and there are now specific scientific studies proving these benefits. The therapeutic value of drumming is also gaining great recognition. Youth and adults, people with disabilities, people experiencing ADHD, and people in recovery, all benefit from the powerful yet simple experience of group rhythm. *(See the Health Rhythms section at www.remo.com for a fantastic overview of these breakthrough studies.)*

Hospitals, schools, and prisons are becoming increasingly aware of the healing, soothing, and educational value of rhythm, song, and dance. All ages experience the neurological and physical benefits that come from participating in rhythm and movement circles. Rhythm bridges cultural boundaries and brings people together. It's not just fun; it really *is* good for us! In many rhythm experiences, I've watched as hundreds of people feel the magic, cut loose, and light up in ways they've never before experienced.

Using this Book

This is an ever-evolving collection of activities using various, easy-to-find rhythm instruments. They are perfect for use in team building and music therapy sessions, classroom learning (making learning really fun) and for conference energizers. The activities fit almost any age; if a participant can firmly hold a stick and use it to hit another object in a regular pattern, they can do just about all of these activities. The activities are broken down into instrument-specific sections. Some activities will crossover; that is, you can use various instruments for the same activity. Activities that defied a specific category are found in the **Multi-Instrument Games** chapter of the book (pg. 93).

You don't have to be a musician to facilitate these activities. As I mentioned earlier, anyone and everyone has rhythm. While practice helps (as with anything) there are some simple techniques for immediate rhythm creation. In the second section, you'll get lots of tips on instant rhythm creation. If you want to take your rhythm facilitation to the highest level, read the book *Drum Circle Spirit* by Arthur Hull, the Granddaddy of drum circle facilitation. Or better yet, check out one of his dynamic trainings. You can find more of his information at www.drumcircle.com.

I suggest that you try these activities yourself before you do them with a group (unless it's a group of facilitators and you are experimenting). Give yourself some practice, and minimize the uncomfortable element of surprise that can occur when an activity does not go the way you intended. The activities are written in a very kinesthetic manner; you'll better understand the directions if you actually get up and try them as you read.

Certain activities in the Sticks, Boomwhackers® tuned percussion tubes, and Sound Shapes® sections are sequenced. That is, the skills and challenges build from one activity to the next in specific order. To get the most out of these activities, I recommend having your group do the first activity in each sequence before moving to the next.

Feel free to modify as you go; I encourage you to explore and play around with the ideas here, and let me know what you create. The world of rhythm is indeed infinite, and can provide hours of very interesting activities, so play, play, play! That's really what this is all about.

Skills Index

Besides the opportunity to play and have fun, these activities can be used to develop or practice specific skills in leadership, group cohesion, and affective skills enhancement (active listening, clear communication etc.). The **Activity Skills Index** on page 133, lists the primary skill focus for each activity, the challenge level, and the appropriate age group for each activity. The index is a great reference for matching an activity with a group.

Challenge Level

The activities range in challenge level from 0 to 5. A challenge level of "0" means the activity is very easy to facilitate and easy for participants to do with little explanation. These are great energizers, warm-up or quick transition activities. A challenge level of "5" means there is more facilitation required and thus more skill building during the activity. These are great for problem solving and focused team building, and you may want to debrief the experience to reinforce learning. Regardless of the challenge level, each activity can be modified to make it easier or more difficult depending on your group's needs.

Variations

In the **Variations** section of each activity, you will find ways to extend an activity as well as suggestions for adding challenges. These suggestions can often provide insights for making the activity unique to your group and situation, and can increase the versatility of an activity.

Equipment

For equipment all you need are the instruments covered in the book (egg shakers, sticks, Boomwhackers®, and Sound Shapes®) plus a large cowbell or jam block (see page 17). Quantity depends on your budget and group size. Instrument details are covered at the beginning of each section.

Celebrate!

Throughout the activities, you'll notice instructions to celebrate. This is important. When you praise and acknowledge individual or group accomplishments it keeps the spirit of rhythm and play alive. Rhythm and music making can sometimes feel risky for participants, so consistent, supportive encouragement invites even the shyest person to jump in and experience the groove. Celebration feeds the soul of exploration.

Play Activities

If you've never facilitated group play activities, (and even if you have), you may want to explore other books and training methods (not necessarily rhythm based, but still totally fun). They will help you practice the "play" mind. Some of my all time favorites are by Chris Cavert (www.fundoing.com) and Sam Sikes (www.learningunlimited.com). Their websites are definitely worth a visit. More information is available in the **Resources** section on page 119.

More Training

All the activities in this book can be experienced in single- or multiple-day training sessions led by Source Consulting Groups's facilitators. Training sessions are one of the best ways to fully understand the power and joy inherent in Rhythm Play.

Enjoy, keep groovin', and keep in touch!
kenya@sourceconsultinggroup.com
kenya@rhythmoflifedrumming.com

Everybody has rhythm.

Formations

"Every time a group of kids or a community sits down and creates rhythmical synergy together, the world is a better place."
Arthur Hull, Drum Circle Spirit

FORMATIONS

Each activity has a specific formation that makes the rhythmic experience flow. Review these before you jump into the activities so you can facilitate with more clarity. The formations assume that participants will be standing; for sitting you may need to make simple modifications.

CONGLOMERATE

In this formation, the group can stand randomly, facing the facilitator with enough space between each participant so they can move their arms without hitting a neighbor.

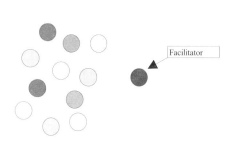

LARGE CIRCLE

Everyone stands in the circle so you can see each person's eyes. Adjust the space as needed for comfortable body movements and/or swinging drumsticks. The facilitator may be part of the circle or stand outside the circle, depending on the activity and the number of participants. If you are working with limited space, set up two independent circles and have participants stand as close together as is comfortable or appropriate.

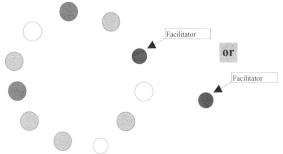

CONCENTRIC CIRCLES

This is very similar to the *Large Circle* formation except that there are two circles: one inner and one outer. The inner circle participants face the outer circle participants and line up with a partner from the outer circle. This works best with even-numbered groups. The facilitator may be part of a circle or stand outside the circles, depending on the number of people needed for the activity.

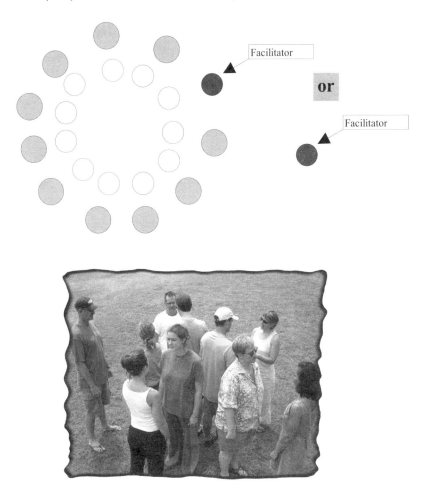

PARALLEL LINES

The group is split evenly into two, and participants stand facing each other in two lines.

Depending on the activity and number of participants, the facilitator may be part of a line or stand at an end.

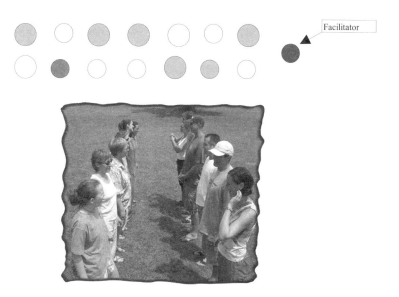

Facilitator

STAGGERED LINES

The group is split evenly into two lines. Participants stand facing the facilitator so that those in the back line do not have a person in the front line blocking their view.

Facilitator

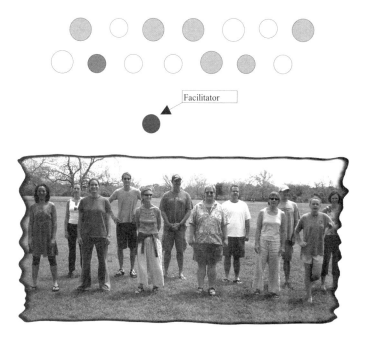

SMALL GROUPS

Depending on the size of your entire group, small groups might consist of 3 to 6 people. Have small groups locate themselves in different parts of the room so they can work as undisturbed as possible for small group activities. They may utilize any other formation within their small groups to help them accomplish tasks. The facilitator moves around the room, offering any necessary support to each group.

Facilitator moves around room

SINGE-FILE LINE

This is a standard single file line. Depending on the activity, partici-pants may stand shoulder to shoulder or facing the back of the person in front of them. The facilitator stands as part of the line or wherever participants can see (or hear) her.

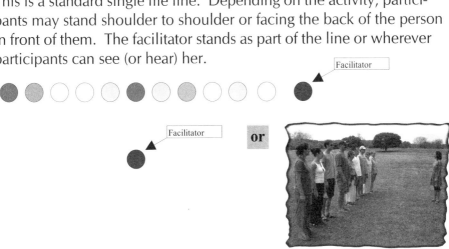

Facilitator

Facilitator

or

13

Play and explore...

Connecting with Rhythm

"Rhythm is the soul of life. The whole universe revolves in rhythm. Everything and every human action revolves in rhythm."

Baba Olatunji

OVERVIEW

O.K; so you've always wanted to play a rhythm instrument and maybe felt somewhat intimidated. Or maybe you are a virtuoso and just need a few more ideas for working with groups. That's what this section is about: finding grooves. They're all over the place...really! Grooves are *everywhere*.

The first thing to keep in mind is that a rhythm is simply a repeated pattern. Even a simple repeated pattern has much merit, as long as it stays connected to a **Pulse**. I describe the Pulse as the basic feel or count of a rhythm (for most Western music it's: 1-2-3-4 / 1-2-3-4 etc.). If you listen to any song on the radio and clap your hands or tap your feet to the beat, you've found the Pulse.

I often ask a group (rhetorically), "What happens to you if *you* don't have a Pulse?" Pretty obvious answer; folks usually shake their heads or say, "That's not so good..." I'll also ask, "What happens to you if *your* Pulse is not steady, or if it's weak or erratic?" Again, the answer is obvious, "You can't stand up." "You're in bad shape." "You'd be weak." It's the same thing with a rhythm; the Pulse has to be strong and steady to keep the rhythm or groove alive.

Now, who's responsible for the Pulse? Usually, the group points to me and laughs! But eventually it becomes clear: each person in the circle is responsible for keeping the Pulse and thus the groove, alive. It's part of the unspoken responsibility we take on when we make rhythm together. It's part of the unspoken lesson of community and team building that happens in any rhythm circle. To support your group, however, a facilitator should have handy either a large cowbell or a jam block (see pictures). These instruments are usually loud enough to be heard over the other instruments and are good for supporting the Pulse.

That leads to the last bit of wisdom around instant rhythm: *listening*. The way to keep the Pulse alive is to listen. As a skill, active listening is hard to teach. In rhythm experiences, the lesson teaches itself. It's essential to have a group simply play a Pulse to understand and de-velop this important skill (see the activity called **The Pulse** on page 20).

Another basic rhythm skill is called a **4-count stop**. Once you get the groove going, it's fun to know how to get everyone to stop together. Simply count 4 Pulses in the *tempo* (the speed of playing), and say or signal, "Stop," on the 5th Pulse. E.G.:

The Pulse: 1-2-3-4, 1-2-3-4 (etc.); Then the stop: "1-2-3-4-Stop!"

You can also use a count to start playing. I usually count 3 Pulses, then say, "And," on the 4th Pulse; instruments kick in on what would be 5:

"1-2-3-and go!" *(Play starts on "go;" you can use a hand motion to signal it).*

It's beneficial to clarify starts and stops so the group feels unified. It also adds to the enjoyment.

To sum it all up, all you need to make rhythm is a willingness to *listen* for the *Pulse* and keep it alive. Rock on.

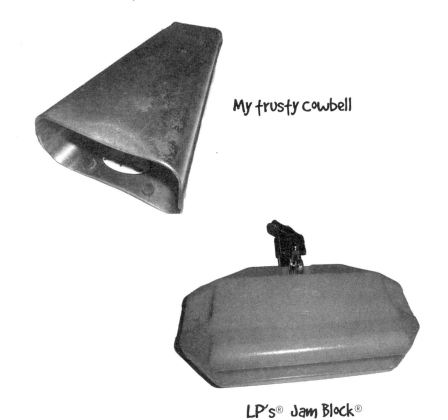

My trusty cowbell

LP's® Jam Block®

Brain Rhythm

GROUP SIZE
Minimum: 4
Maximum: 40+
Challenge Level: 0

TIME
10 minutes; longer if you are working with younger children

INSTRUMENTS
None; just the body

FORMATION
Large Circle or Staggered Lines

INSTRUCTIONS

1) Get the group to stand in a large circle or staggered lines so that the entire group can easily see you. Let everyone know that getting loose makes the jam, *JAM!* A "jam" happens when everyone grooves together.

2) Explain that *breathing* is the most important part of this activity. You may get some chuckles and stares. However, it's true; participants will need to remember to focus on the rhythm of their breath to get through the activity. Also encourage participants to find their own rhythm. They can go as slow or as fast as is comfortable to them. This activity is not about keeping up with other participants; it's about finding their own Pulse, so there won't be a specific group Pulse kept during the activity. The movements purposely cross the left-right planes of the body, or activate the left and right limbs independently; this stimulates the left and right brain integration.

3) While standing in place, begin crossing and uncrossing your legs in front of you (left across right, right across left, etc.). Ask the group to do the same so that everyone is doing the movement together. Tell the group to focus on breathing. Coordinating breathing with moving, helps each person find their rhythm.

4) After a few moments instruct the participants to start swinging their arms front to back (like a robot walking, only not so stiff). *Keep the feet moving at same time!* Now there should be more laughter as folks simultaneously integrate both movements while focusing on breathing. Give them lots of encouragement as there's more coming.

5) After a few moments, add heads turning left and right while feet cross and arms move front to back. *Remind them to breathe!* The breath keeps them connected to their rhythm.

6) Next, ask them to begin wiggling their fingers and toes with everything else still moving. *Remember the breath!*

7) Finally, invite participants to add blinking their eyes rapidly...seriously! It's a riot, and folks get a kick out of trying to do all these simultaneous movements. Don't forget to cheer them on (if you can cheer while *you* are performing all the movements as well).

8) Count to four and say, "Stop" (a *4-count stop: 1-2-3-4-stop!*). Have everyone raise their arms up and stretch high, hold the breath for a moment while stretching, then relax down with an exhale. Add another round of the same or add new movements that you create.

NOTES

This activity is about left and right brain integration. It's a key to successful rhythm experiences, so I often use it as a starter. For younger or novice participants, keep your initial instructions simple. As the group gets comfortable, add more complex movements. You are only limited by your comfort and imagination, so improvise, experiment, and have fun with this!

VARIATIONS

Make up your own movements, and be as creative as you can. Practice a few before you try them with a group. Be sure to have the movements cross the left-right planes of the body, or activate the left and right limbs independently. For adventurous groups, integrate getting down on the floor (sitting or laying) for more movements. Also, have small groups of 3 to 4 people create movements for the entire group to try.

The Pulse

GROUP SIZE
Minimum: 4
Maximum: 40+
Challenge Level: 0

TIME
5 to 10 minutes; longer if you choose

INSTRUMENTS
Anything you have available (bells, Sound Shapes®, Boomwhackers®, shakers etc.)
You could consider clapping, but it makes hands sore if it goes on for too long. The facilitator should use an instrument that can be heard above the group (a cowbell or jam block).

FORMATION
Large Circle or Conglomerate for smaller spaces

INSTRUCTIONS
1) Play a slow Pulse on any instrument you have: 1-2-3-4 / 1-2-3-4 etc.

2) Invite the group to join in and keep the Pulse. Inevitably, it will speed up without you doing anything. Stop the group as soon as this happens, and ask them what they heard. Someone will probably say, "We sped up!" The rest of the group will usually agree. You continue, "That's good to notice; it means we're listening." Let them know they're about to do the same thing (play just the Pulse), but this time their challenge is to keep the Pulse at the tempo (speed) you began: no speeding up and no slowing down.

3) Start the Pulse again, and ask the group to join in. The facilitator's job is to hold on to the original Pulse no matter what. It's great practice!

4) After a short while you'll feel the group lock into the Pulse. Cheer them on! Now let them know you are going to time the Pulse; their task is to hold an even Pulse for one minute without you (the facilitator) playing. If they waver, alert them with a motion, sound, or funny facial expression, and see if they can bring it back on.

If not, you can jump in to get it back on track. If it totally falls apart, it's a great opportunity to discuss listening and team cooperation. Try to get that full minute in before moving to the next step. Always cheer them on!

5) If the group is still into it, start the Pulse again. Once everyone is locked in, say, "Let's speed up slowly." Let it speed up and then ask them to hold the Pulse when you feel it's at a good tempo. Speed up again and hold. Now slow down. If the group is listening, you'll begin to notice that the tempo changes happen almost simultaneously; this is real synergy. Start and stop a few times so the group can practice following tempo changes. Use a few variations to complete the activity.

NOTES

This activity gets the group to listen and tune into each other and the Pulse. It's another great introductory activity and can be done with no previous rhythm experience. Your primary task as facilitator is to keep a strong and constant Pulse at whatever tempo you have chosen.

VARIATIONS

Let other members lead the tempo changes. What do you notice in the group dynamics when different people lead? Also, how fast or how slow can the group maintain (the key here is *maintain*) a clear Pulse. Can they come up with strategies to keep themselves on Pulse? This is great for community building.

Everyone can do it!

Rhythm in the Kitchen

GROUP SIZE
Minimum: 4
Maximum: 40 +
Challenge Level: 1

TIME
5 to 10 minutes; longer if you choose.

INSTRUMENTS
Anything you have available; voices and clapping will work if you have no instruments.
The facilitator should use an instrument that can be heard above the group (cowbell or jam block).

FORMATION
Large Circle, then Small Groups *(variation)*

INSTRUCTIONS
1) Tell the group you are going to build a "rhythm-peanut-butter-and-jelly sandwich. I often ask, "What's the first thing you need?" Some folks say the peanut butter, but I'm not sure how to start a sandwich with just peanut butter, so I start with bread. I then ask folks what type of bread they would like to use. The answer is usually white or wheat, and that's the rhythm pattern for the bread: *white-or-whole-wheat*. Or you can just choose one flavor: *whole-wheat-bread* (more fun for the rhythm than just playing "*white-bread*").

If you emphasize (chant) the syllables of white-or-whole-wheat, or whole-wheat-bread, you get a nice simple rhythm.

E.g.:   *White-or-whole-wheat*: there are 4 syllables here that create a rhythm pattern.
Whole-wheat-bread: there are 3 syllables here that create a rhythm pattern.

If you tap your feet to the syllables while you chant it, you'll hear the pattern.

2) Using instruments and voices, play call-and-response with the group (you play a pattern and say the chant, they echo it back also saying the chant). You may want to start each rhythm that way. (See **Call and Response** in the Sticks section on **pg. 43** for more on this idea.)

3) Once the group has this groove pattern down (the *Pulse* is inherent in the groove), it's time to add the next ingredient to the sandwich. Have the group chant the words "spread peanut butter," or just "peanut butter." Again, emphasize the syllables to make it rhythmic (spread-pea-nut-bu-tter). Practice until the group has it down.

4) Split the circle in half by designating two sides. You'll designate the sides by motioning; the people will stay as they are in one large circle. One side will be the bread, the other the peanut butter. Their challenge will be to play their rhythms on instruments and keep the patterns in sync. Encourage participants to say the words to help keep them in the groove.

Start the bread group, and then bring in the peanut butter group; the groups (sections of the circle) will be simultaneously chanting and playing their parts. As facilitator, keep the Pulse on your instrument so there is a point of reference. If they can keep the two parts going, stop them after about a minute; stop sooner if it falls apart. Practice it a few times.

5) If they've got that, add the third ingredient, the jelly! (If not, work with more simple combinations of patterns.) Strawberry is my favorite, and it's a great rhythm (straw-be-rry-je-lly). Divide the circle into three sections, and assign a rhythm to each section. Always start with the bread, as it's closer to the Pulse, then add the peanut butter, then the jelly.

Here are the rhythms:
   1) *White-or-whole-wheat,* or *whole-wheat-bread*
   2) *Spread-pea-nut-bu-tter* or just *Pea-nut-bu-tter*
   3) *Straw-be-rry-je-lly*
Once all the parts get going simultaneously, you should have a really cool vocal PBJ groove...nice!

6) Let the three parts play as long as it sounds good and is still fun for participants (watch and feel the energy). You can keep the Pulse going, or assist any of the parts that need a "reminder." End with a *4-count stop.* Celebrate the successful groove! If the group is up for it, try a few variations; it's fun to hear the mixing of rhythms that can happen with the voice.

NOTES

This activity utilizes rhythmic syllables in words. Once you understand how to do this, you are in with the groove! You can use just about anything to create rhythms (even people's names: ken-ya-ma-sa-la). The possibilities for play are limitless.

VARIATIONS

What other recipes have great words? Pizza? Pasta? Use recipes that have lots of fun ingredients; there are endless choices available. For kids, throw in funny food combinations like "sar-dines-and-to-fu" (yum). For more ideas, you'll find some rhythm recipes **(pg. 131)** in the resource section for you to try. If you have a large group, you can split into small groups of 4 to 6 people and have each person in each of the groups create a chant. Can they keep the groove when each person is chanting simultaneously?

For another variation, choose an instrument (or instruments) to play at specific times during a chant. For example, have only bells or small Sound Shapes® play when a word in the chant begins with the letter "p."

Pea-nut-but-ter: The bells would play on "pea" or "pea-nut."

Play-in'-loud-mu-sic-in-the-paw-paw-patch: The bells would play on "play," "paw-paw," and "patch."

You can create different arrangements with other instruments as well. Bells could play on "p" words and shakers play on "m" words. Use your imagination and invite the group's imagination. Make it as simple or as complex as the group can handle...starting with simple is *always* good.

Rhythm Eggs

"…without the obstacle of a challenging learning curve, group [rhythm] is an enjoyable, accessible and fulfilling activity from the start for young and old alike."
Karl Bruhn, Father of the Music-Making and Wellness Movement

OVERVIEW

Rhythm eggs are great instruments. They're inexpensive and so easy to carry that you can have them available for just about any situation. Eggs are also way easy to play...in fact, they almost play themselves. Companies like LP®, Meinl®, and Rhythm Tech® make great eggs, and they are all pretty much the same in size and quality. REMO®, makes fun small shakers called Fruit Shakes® and Veggie Shakes®. From the names, you can imagine what these look like. Check your local music store for egg shakers; they are really easy to find. On-line sources are listed in the resource section.

It's also really easy to make your own egg shakers. Hollow, plastic Easter eggs are sold in various sizes and colors at large art supply and craft stores. They are made so you can fill them with whatever you choose, and then snap them back together. They're really inexpensive, and if you get them right after Easter, you can buy a dozen for as little as $0.50! Have fun exploring the types of fill you use in the eggs (my favorite is popcorn – before it's popped). I recommend gluing the eggshells together at the seams so they don't explode with vigorous play.

A caveat: there are some brands of these eggs made from a soft plastic. I have yet to find glue that will hold them together, so I recommend using thin strips of duct tape glued around the seam with super glue. It sounds unnecessary to glue the tape, but it *will* keep the eggs together and prevent the tape from premature peeling. Do this ahead of time and *NOT* with kids or participants.

Once filled, it's fun to have players try to guess what's inside the eggs as part of your first activity.

Note: I recommend getting a "stuff sack" from a camping supply store to keep your small shakers or eggs. This makes them easy to store and travel.

All right, let's shake it up!

Shake the eggs

GROUP SIZE
Minimum: 1
Maximum: 40 +
Challenge Level: 0

TIME
5 minutes

INSTRUMENTS
One egg or similar small shaker (a film canisters with popcorn works well) per participant. They should be easy to hold in the palm of the hand.

FORMATION
Large Circle or Conglomerate

INSTRUCTIONS
1) Hand one egg to each participant (or hold open your egg bag so each person can grab one). Encourage participants to "play" their egg as soon as they have one (i.e., tell them to go ahead and play it rather than just hold it and wait; shaking is great!). If they all get into it, call a 4-count stop before moving on.

2) For this activity, call out physical movements that can be done with the eggs. For example, "Shake your egg up high!" Hold your egg above your head and shake it; participants copy your actions. "Shake your egg behind your head." Again, do the action and have participants imitate your action. "Shake your egg behind your neighbor's head." You get the idea. Explore, improvise, and have fun here; make up silly ways and places to shake the eggs.

3) Keep this up as long as energy is high (but not so long that participants get bored). When you feel ready to end it, have folks hold their eggs in the middle of the circle and shake them as vigorously as possible. Say, "Faster, louder, faster!" Then count to four, jump up in the air and yell, "Stop!" This is a great way to end and it gets the group tuned to the 4-count stop you'll use for many other activities.

NOTES

For younger participants, be sure the shakers you use can easily fit their hands so they can hold them as they shake, especially with vigorous shaking. Keep your initial instructions simple to begin with and as the group gets comfortable, add more detailed ways to shake the eggs. You are only limited by your imagination.

VARIATIONS

Go around the circle (if the group is not too large) and have each person create a shakin' move for the group to imitate.

"Shake your eggs behind your neighbor's head!"

Eggs Up, Eggs Down

GROUP SIZE
Minimum: 8
Maximum: 40+
Challenge Level: 0

TIME
5 minutes

INSTRUMENTS
One or two egg shakers per person; other small palm sized shakers will work

FORMATION
Large Circle or Conglomerate

INSTRUCTIONS
For this activity, we shake our eggs in the spirit of Simon Says.

1) Start the group shaking with a relatively slow Pulse so that everyone plays together.

2) When you say "Eggs up," raise your egg above your head and continue to shake it in the Pulse, and have the group copy your actions. When you say, "Eggs down," hold your egg low to the ground, keeping the Pulse, and the group should do the same. Call out more positions: behind head, next to right ear, under chin, over neighbors right toes, etc. Always say the word "eggs" before you say the position you want them to do.

3) If you just say, "next to left ear," without saying the word "eggs," whoever makes that move gets a point; go for the lowest personal score.

NOTES
Remember to keep the Pulse going with the group for the entire game. Have fun trying to "fake out" the last person left!

VARIATIONS

If appropriate, let anyone who "messes up" lose the use of a limb (whichever they choose) instead of stepping out. Eventually they may have to hold the egg in their lap, or who knows where! Speed up the Pulse after a couple of slow rounds.

"Eggs up!"

Eggstremely Quiet

GROUP SIZE
Minimum: 3
Maximum: 40+
Challenge Level: 1

TIME
5 to 10 minutes

INSTRUMENTS
One egg or small shaker per person; shakers should be easy to hold in the palm of the hand.
You'll also need another instrument (like a cow bell or jam block) for the Pulse Master.

FORMATION
Single-File Line *(everyone facing the front)*

INSTRUCTIONS

1) Have everyone take an egg. Ask for a volunteer to be the *Pulse Master*. This person uses the other loud instrument, and is allowed to move around the playing area.

2) Set up two parallel boundary lines, with at least 20 to 30 feet in between them. All egg holders start behind the first boundary line. The object is to be the first to cross the second boundary line without shaking your egg (or at least without being *heard* shaking your egg).

3) Players start by holding an egg in a closed fist, then fully extending that arm. They'll keep this position for the entire game. They must stand at least two feet away from their neighbor. When the *Pulse Master* hits a beat, all players take a step. How large a step? Remember the object of the game! If the *Pulse Master* hears an egg at all, she will point that person back to the starting position to begin again. The Pulse played by the *Pulse Master* must be soft enough so she can hear any noise the egg shakers may make.

NOTES

What if outstretched arms get tired? As long as a player can switch hands without being heard, that's O.K. If you have a large group, you may want to have more than one *Pulse Master*. One will hit the Pulse, while others move around the room and listen.

VARIATIONS

You can lengthen the distance between the boundary lines if you have a group that's really into the activity. Also, with a slow Pulse, have participants try moving with their eyes closed. For an extra challenge, each time a person is pointed out, they become part of the *Pulse Master's* team, and have to listen for others making sounds.

"Hang on to that egg..."

Amoebeggs

GROUP SIZE
Minimum: 10
Maximum: 40+
Challenge Level: 1

TIME
15 minutes

INSTRUMENTS
Two egg shakers per person; other small instruments like bells or jingles will work just as well.

FORMATION
Small Groups

INSTRUCTIONS
1) Separate the large group into small groups of 3 to 6 people depending on the size of the large group.

2) The task for each group is to keep a Pulse or rhythmic flow going while moving. Sounds easy? Great! Then you tell them that they have to move as a unified team, with people physically connected in some way. They could link arms, legs, or whatever they choose; they just have move as a unit.

3) Choose a starting and ending line for the small groups and have them make their moves one group at a time. If they loose the groove, or disconnect, they have to start again.

NOTES
This is a fun activity to do after groups have had some Pulse and simple rhythm practice.

VARIATIONS
You can add some fun competition here by having the groups race from start to finish (or by timing each group for best time). Keep the same rules of maintaining the groove and staying physically connected. Groups can also add dance steps for style points!

Take it, Pass it (Adapted from Barry Bernstein)

GROUP SIZE
Minimum: 4
Maximum: 40+
Challenge Level: 2

TIME
30 minutes; possibly longer if your group is large or you are working with younger children

INSTRUMENTS
One egg or similar small shaker per participant; the shakers should be easy to hold in the palm of the hand.

FORMATION
Large Circle

INSTRUCTIONS
1) Hand one egg to each participant. Encourage each person to explore shaking their egg as soon as they get one.

2) Once everyone has a shaker, ask the group to watch you. I usually pretend I am teaching a magic trick to make the skill building session fun and silly (you can create your own script).
"Behold, I have an egg in my left hand!" I hold the egg up high in my left hand.
I say the magic words, "One, two, three, take an egg!" On the word "take," I take the egg from my left and into my right hand, then continue speaking, "And voila, the egg is now in my right hand!"
Participants give me all kinds of silly looks here. Anyway, you get the idea; it's a simple pass from the left to the right hand, and participants should do as you've done.

3) Invite everyone to practice. First, everyone holds an egg in his or her left hand, and then all say the words together in rhythm, "One-two-three-***take***-an-egg."

4) Each person should now have their egg in the right hand. This time, ask them to leave left hands extended toward their left neighbor after taking the egg. Ask each person to look to their right and notice their neighbor's left hand ready to receive an egg.

5) Have the group relax as you demonstrate the next step with your neighbor. Start the egg in your left again, and say, "One-two-three-***take***-an-egg" and transfer the egg from your left to your right hand. Then say, "One-two-three-***pass***-an-egg," and on the word "pass," place the egg into your neighbor's outstretched left hand.

6) Now set the group up to try it once. The eggs will flow from a person's left hand to their right, and then to their neighbor's left. Emphasize the rhythm of words as you do each step. Say, "Ready!" Check to make sure all eggs are in the left hand. Then, "One-two-three-***take***-an-egg." Pause for a moment to make sure the switch happened) then, "One-two-three-***pass***-an-egg. Everyone should now have his or her neighbor's egg.

7) Now work in a fluid motion, nice and slow to keep the egg pass happening around the circle. Always say, "Ready!" and hold the egg in your left hand to get the group set. Then, "One-two-three-***take***-an-egg; one-two-three-***pass***-an-egg." Stop to make sure everyone's got it, then again, "One-two-three-***take***-an-egg; one-two-three-***pass***-an-egg."

8) As the group gets into a nice flow, let them know you are going to change the spoken rhythm to "One-two-***take***-an-egg, one-two-***pass***-an-egg." (Now you are only counting to two.) Do a few rounds with this, then change to just a one count, "One-***take***-an-egg, one-***pass***-an-egg."

9) Finally, no counting; simply say, "***Take***-an-egg, ***pass***-an-egg." Keep the eggs going around the circle, while the group chants in rhythm as they pass the eggs. If an egg drops, don't stop to pick it up, just have them go on, pretending to pass the egg until too many have fallen to keep going. The challenge is for them to work together in the rhythm so that the eggs move smoothly around the circle without being dropped. This adds a nice element of team problem solving.

10) End the activity when the group has successfully gotten all the eggs around the circle at least once without a drop, then celebrate!

NOTES

This is a fantastic team activity. It utilizes the cooperative principle while incorporating rhythm and listening. Remind the group that tuning into the rhythm is the foundation that gets all team members on the same page. For younger participants, be sure the shakers you use can fit easily in their hands so that they can hang on to them as they make passes. Because of the left-right instructions, this is sometimes tough for preschool and kindergarten children to do without a lot of help. Enthusiastically remind the group to say the words with you to support the Pulse and rhythm.

VARIATIONS

Once the group is comfortable taking and passing have them take and pass in silence; they can say the words if they need to, just not out loud. Try varying the tempo; see how fast the group can go without dropping eggs. Ask the group how they feel the tempo might be related to their team's process?

Have the team close their eyes and pass eggs. That's often a lot of fun, with some surprising responses.

You can add an "under leg" to the take and pass sequence. It would sound like this: "*Take*-an-egg-*un-der*-leg," (pass from left to right hand under a lifted leg on the word "under") "*hold*-an-egg," (hold it up high in the right hand) "*pass*-an-egg," (pass to neighbor as before). Remember, whatever motions you use should fit the flow of a rhythm and a Pulse.

Here's the whole sequence:
1) *Take*-an-egg-un-der-leg
2) *Hold*-an-egg
3) *Pass*-an-egg

Finally, when the team is good at passing eggs from left to right, yell out "Reverse!" Some good processing questions might be, "How does this affect the team process?" "How quickly can the team build the skills for passing eggs in the other direction?"

Take an egg...

Pass an egg...

Egg Drop Soup

GROUP SIZE
Minimum: 8
Maximum: 40+ *You'll need an even-numbered group.*
Challenge Level: 3

TIME
10 to 15 minutes

INSTRUMENTS
One egg or similar small shaker per person; use shakers that are easy to hold in the palm of the hand.

FORMATION
Concentric Circles

INSTRUCTIONS
This is a great follow up activity to **Take it, Pass it**.

1) Once you've got a group that's mastered the egg pass, divide them into two even groups, forming concentric circles. The inner circle will be facing out, and the outer circle facing in; each person should be standing in front of a partner.

2) Starting with passes from left to right (as in **Take it, Pass it**), and get each circle moving eggs around so they reconnect to the Pulse and flow of the rhythm. This is fun as each group sees and hears both theirs *and* the other circle's rhythm. At this point, the inner circle's eggs will be moving clockwise; the outer circle's eggs will be moving counter-clockwise.

3) After a minute or so, encourage both groups to work on the same Pulse (if they've not already done so). This could be a challenge in and of itself!

4) Now for the main challenge of the activity. Tell the groups that their task is to get the eggs moving around both circles, such that eggs are moving from the outer to the inner circles as they travel around. Let them try to figure it out before you intervene or give hints. It's actually easier than it sounds, but it creates a great opportunity for communication, planning, and cooperative efforts to be brought to focus (see notes for more info).

NOTES

This is another great team activity, requiring the participants to call on the principles of community building. I call these the 4 C's: *Communication, Cooperation, Creativity,* and *Compassion.* The solution is to pass the eggs from inner to outer circle, and both circles must be passing either clockwise or counter clockwise. Let the group discover the answer (there are a few ways to do it). See the diagram for one possibility.

VARIATIONS

Use tempo variations, "Reverse!", and closed eyes to add some more challenges.

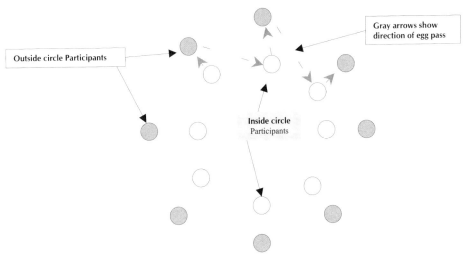

Gray arrows show direction of egg pass

Outside circle Participants

Inside circle Participants

Grab your sticks and here we go!

Drum Sticks

"If you can talk, you can sing; if you can walk, you can dance; if you can clap, you can drum!"
African Proverb

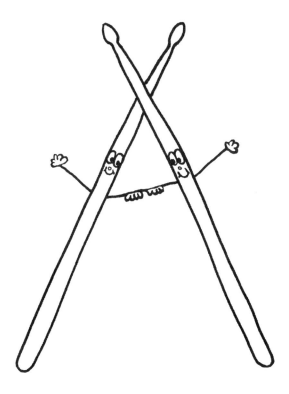

OVERVIEW

If all you had were sticks, you could rock on for days! By sticks, I mean any 10- to 12-inch long cylindrical object with a diameter of ¼ to ½ inch. Wood is best, as it's safe for hitting almost any surface, though some types of plastics may work well (just be sure it doesn't shatter at high impact). Dowels are great since they are readily available at hardware stores. Dowels *will* tend to splinter pretty easily if hit against hard surfaces so inspect them after each use.

Bona fide drumsticks work best, being designed for impact. They tend to take much more abuse before they splinter, and there is a mystique to real drumsticks that makes them immediately engaging. They can be a bit expensive so look for the sales. Local music stores sometimes have buckets of sticks on sale. Large stores like American Music Academy or Guitar Center have great sales from time to time and will usually help schools with discounts on bulk orders. The best deals I've found are on line at www.musiciansfriend.com. Look or ask for their promotional drumsticks.

For working with younger children, bulk chopsticks can be found for great prices at Asian markets. I recommend the plastic variety, as bamboo will splinter. You can sometimes find larger sizes of the plastic chopsticks, which give a little more of a satisfying "umph" when hit. Keep in mind that chopsticks really work best for younger children. Wrapping rubber bands in balls around the ends of chopsticks turns them into small mallets and enhances their "bangability."

Again, I recommend getting a large enough "stuff sack" from a camping supply store to keep your sticks together. It makes them easy to store and travel and lasts much longer than a cardboard box.

Here we go, stick time!

Chopstick "Mallets"

Call and Response

GROUP SIZE
Minimum: 2
Maximum: 40+
Challenge Level: 0

TIME
5 to 10 minutes

INSTRUMENTS
1 pair of sticks per person
You can modify good ol' Call and Response to work with any instruments you have.

FORMATION
Large Circle or Conglomerate

INSTRUCTIONS
1) Give each person a pair of sticks. In my experience, the first thing participants usually do is hit each other, so be sure to specify ground rules before you hand them out. You could assign someone to lead a rhythm while the sticks are passed out, providing an activity for the group until you are ready.

2) Once everyone has a pair, get their attention and let them know this will be **call** (*leader plays*) and **response** (*group responds*). I usually say, "I play, then you play." Start out with a very simple pattern like a four count on the sticks. The group responds. Then take it from there, adding to or modifying the call. Depending on the age and experience of your group, you'll want to keep the calls simple, yet not too predictable. That is part of the point of call and response: to keep the group listening.

3) Keep the tempo slow enough so that the group can follow, and only speed it up as the group is able to keep up; you want to keep a sense of unity, not chaos. For some groups, vocalizing the riff (the short rhythm pattern you created) adds another auditory component to the visual and kinesthetic learning styles. Vocalizing simply means adding verbal sounds to the beat of the stick pattern, instead of only playing the pattern on the sticks.

4) Once the group is in a groove and flowing with call and response, you can let them know you are going to add more to your calls to "up the challenge." You can now make your rhythm patterns (riffs) a little longer and more complicated, but again, keep the riffs within your group's ability.

NOTES

The power of call and response should not be underestimated. This simple activity tunes the nervous system and ears to the feel and flow of rhythm. Stop the activity before the interest wanes and the group gets bored. If I am using sticks, I like to go right into **Stick-Stick-Shoe-Floor** (pg. 47) from this activity.

VARIATIONS

As with the eggs, go around the circle (if the group is not too large) and have each person do a call to which the group will respond. You can play with the tempo (speed) as well as volume (dynamics) and add vocalizations to add more interest to your calls.

I play, then you play...

World Tour

GROUP SIZE
Minimum: 3
Maximum: 30
Challenge Level: 0

TIME
10 minutes

INSTRUMENTS
1 pair of sticks per person

FORMATION
Large Circle, then Single-File Line *(facing the back of the person in front)*

INSTRUCTIONS
1) Give each person a pair of sticks. Begin by doing a bit of call and response, and having the group hold a Pulse.

2) Explain that they are going to go on tour. The person on your right (or left) will follow you, and the circle should become a singe-file line. The person on your left (or right depending on where you started the line) will end up being the tail.

3) Begin by playing a Pulse on your sticks and start walking around the room, letting the line get used to following you. Then, as you walk by durable objects, play on them; the rest of the line should do the same. Now you don't have to play a Pulse; you can just jam out on the objects.

4) This is even more exciting if you leave the room and play along walls, doors, drainpipes, railings, floors, etc. Take the group on a walking drumming tour of surfaces in or outside your building. Look for surfaces that will make interesting sounds when your band of drummers comes by to play them.

5) Travel around for whatever time feels appropriate and then lead the group back into the starting room. Walk around in a circle playing the Pulse until everyone is back in sync, and end with a **4-count stop**.

NOTES

Danger! Make sure you choose *durable* things to hit (e.g., desks, chairs, steel railings, etc.), but no windows! Also be sure the surfaces you hit are not doors of other classes in session, or soft walls where the sticks will leave a mark. Also, this is a relatively loud activity (as you can imagine). Don't let this dissuade you from trying it; it's really a blast, and is often one of the most requested activities with youth.

VARIATIONS

Modify the tempo and volume as you "tour" and ask participants to follow. You can also call someone from the middle of the line to lead, and switch out leaders as you move around.

Groove wherever you go!

Stick-Stick-Shoe-floor

GROUP SIZE
Minimum: 2
Maximum: 40 +
Challenge Level: 1

TIME
5 to 10 minutes

INSTRUMENTS
1 pair of sticks per person

FORMATION
Large Standing Circle or Standing Conglomerate

INSTRUCTIONS

1) This is a great follow up to **Call and Response** on **pg. 43**. Once all participants have sticks, play a Pulse and invite everyone to play it with you. Call out a 4-count stop to end the Pulse.

2) Explain that this activity will be like "follow the leader;" say, "I'll play, then you'll play and do whatever I do." Again, start out with a very simple pattern, like a four count played on sticks *(1-2-3-4 and the group responds playing 1-2-3-4)*. Then take it from there, adding to or modifying the call, making a funny face or a body movement as you call out simple rhythms. Do this for about a minute. (Remember to keep the calls and movements simple enough for your particular group to follow, but challenging enough to keep them interested.)

3) Once the group is in the groove, sit down (cross-legged style) so you can hit your sticks together, and also hit the floor. This brings another tone into the pattern, so a simple riff might be: *stick-stick-floor-floor* (the group responds), then you play *stick-floor-stick-floor*, and so on.

Caution: some wooden floors may be marred or scratched by sticks, so test this out in a corner before you start the activity or get permission to hit the floor. Keep the tempo slow enough so that the group can follow, only speeding up as the group can follow; you want to keep a sense of unity, not chaos. For some groups, saying the words *stick* and *floor* when you strike the sticks or floor helps tie the verbal in with the kinesthetic.

4) Now uncross your legs and stick your feet out in front so you can add hits on your shoes. A pattern might be: *stick-stick-shoe-shoe* (hit sticks together twice, then hit your shoes twice); the group responds, copying what you've done. Then try *stick-stick-shoe-floor*. Here's another: *stick-shoe-floor-shoe*, or *stick-stick-floor-floor-shoe-shoe-shoe* and so on. The patterns you create are unlimited (just remember your group's ability). Feel free to explore and play around; it's really fun!

NOTES

This activity takes call and response and group focus to more kinesthetic heights; keep chanting *stick, floor,* or *shoe,* as necessary to keep your group in the groove.

VARIATIONS

Go around the circle (if the group is not too large) and invite each person to create a riff to which the group will respond. Encourage them to integrate their shoes, the floor, and even *(softly!)* tap on a body part (their own, not someone else's!) as part of the rhythm pattern; e.g., *Sticks-floor-shoe-shoe* (group responds), then *sticks-floor-shoe-thighs* (group responds), etc.

You can add a "Simon Says" component to this activity. Remind the group to play what you play, **regardless of what you say**. So if you **say** *stick-shoe-floor-shoe,* but you actually **play** *stick-shoe-stick-shoe,* you'll be able to "fake them out" adding more challenge to the fun (and more reasons to focus). No one has to be "out" if they mess up (unless that would work for your group); it's just a great way to bring more laughs.

The Sound of One (Learned from Chris Cavert)

GROUP SIZE
Minimum: 3
Maximum: 30
Challenge Level: 2

TIME
10 minutes

INSTRUMENTS
1 pair of sticks per person
You can increase the teamwork factor with one stick per person; see variation. Other homogenous instruments or handclaps will work.

FORMATION
Large Circle or Conglomerate

INSTRUCTIONS
1) Give each person a pair of sticks. Tell the group that the challenge here will be to make one sound such that it's not possible to tell that there is more than one person making the sound. This activity is all about synergy and unity.

2) Ask them to make a plan; how will they attempt to coordinate their one sound action? After at least three attempts, ask them if they want to try other possibilities (see variations).

3) When they are successful, have them try more than one sound in a row. How many can they do in rhythm and still keep a unified sound?

NOTES
This is another great teambuilding activity, and includes the concepts of planning, implementing, and restructuring. As the team's plans develop, ask them if they are getting input from all members, or are only a few members directing the process?

VARIATIONS

If each participant has only one stick, you can direct him or her to hit sticks with another participant (more cooperation required) or hit an appropriate object (e.g., the floor).

The Sound of Unity...

Sticky Situation

GROUP SIZE
Minimum: 4
Maximum: 30
This works best with small subgroups; if you have a large group, divide them up into smaller groups of 4 to 5 people max.
Challenge Level: 2

TIME
15 minutes

INSTRUMENTS
1 pair of sticks per person
Boomwhackers® Tuned Percussion Tubes or Sound Shapes® can also be used.

FORMATION
Small Groups in "Large Circle" formation

INSTRUCTIONS
1) This is a rhythm memory game, so groups should be no larger than 6 people. Choose a person to start (or you can be the starting person). Play a simple rhythm pattern with your sticks (like the rhythm that goes with *"I-like-je-lly-beans"*).

2) The person to your right (or left, however you want to move around the circle) must play your rhythm, and add their own simple rhythm to it.

3) The next person must play both your rhythm and the rhythm that was just added, and then add one of their own. It continues with the next person until you've got a long sequence for the last person to play (yikes!).

NOTES
Keep this fun by recommending that the added rhythms be simple for the first round. As you can imagine, this could get really hard for the last person in the circle, so keep it fun and easy. Depending on the skill level, you may want to keep the groups to a maximum of 3 to 4 people. Also encourage the group to develop ways to support each teammate in remembering the rhythms (like adding vocalizations etc.).

VARIATIONS

Instead of each person around the circle playing solo, you can have the entire group play back the rhythms *and* each addition. Each person still gets to add a rhythm, but it becomes the whole group's task to play through the sequence. Add vocalizations or body movements for more challenge and fun. This can also be done in twos; two people create a simple rhythm pattern (both playing the same pattern), then the next two people in the circle add to it and so on.

Listen closely...then play it back!

My Sticks, Your Sticks

GROUP SIZE
Minimum: 8
Maximum: 30 *You'll need an even-numbered group for this activity.*
Challenge Level: 3

TIME
20 minutes

INSTRUMENTS
1 pair of sticks per person
*Boomwhackers® Tuned Percussion Tubes can also be used.
The facilitator should use an instrument that can be heard above the group (a cowbell or jam block).*

FORMATION
Large Circle then Concentric Circles

INSTRUCTIONS
1) Starting in a circle, give each person a pair of sticks. Play a Pulse to get the group connected and hold it for at least a minute. Remind the group that the Pulse will be the anchor for the activity.

2) Divide the group in half, forming concentric circles. Ask the folks on the inner circle to find a partner on the outer circle and stand in front of that person; you should have concentric circles with the participants facing each other.

3) Demonstrate the following safety feature of this activity. Ask all those on the outside circle to hold their sticks horizontally, gripping the sticks at the far ends, and the points of the sticks touching in front. Those on the inside circle will hold their sticks vertically. Partners play each other's sticks; they are held this way so fingers do not get hit (see the picture on the next page). Remind them that each partner is actively playing the other's sticks, not just holding them up for the partner to hit.

Stick positions

4) Tell the group that a chant as well as the sticks will carry the Pulse. Do a demonstration with a participant or with your partner. The chant goes, "*My sticks,*" and hit your own sticks together on the beat of the syllables. Then chant, "*Your sticks,*" and play your partner's sticks on the beat of the syllables as she plays yours.

5) Ask each pair to try it, chanting, "*My-sticks-your-sticks-my-sticks-your sticks,* and so on, keeping the Pulse with sticks and chanting. The whole group should lock into the cadence and chant; practice it a few times until everyone's together.

6) If you did this for longer than 30 seconds, you may notice the group speed up the tempo, totally ignoring the original Pulse. I'll point it out to them just so they can be aware of it, and bring focus back to staying with the Pulse. I also encourage them to keep it slow for now, as I'll be adding things for them to do. Try it again just for Pulse practice (keep the Pulse with the cowbell or jam block).

7) Now we'll add more! Tell the outer circle to stay as they are, and ask the inner circle to step to the right as they play sticks. Demonstrate with a participant or your partner. "*My-sticks-your-sticks-step-step-step-step.*"

You'll start off as before, hitting your sticks twice, (my-sticks) and then your partner's sticks twice (your-sticks), then take 4 steps to the right (hit sticks together with each step) and arrive in front of a new partner (the person to your right on the *outer* circle). Take a look at the diagram.

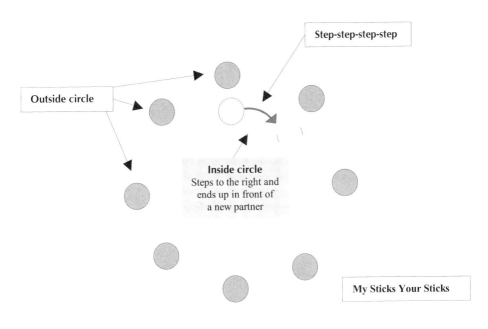

Step-step-step-step

Outside circle

Inside circle
Steps to the right and
ends up in front of
a new partner

My Sticks Your Sticks

8) Have folks line up with partners again. Let them know you will use verbal cues to help them out at this phase, and ask them to wait until you tell them to step. First get them all on the my-sticks-your-sticks Pulse. Start by counting the Pulse so they all hear and feel it. *"One, two, three, four, my-sticks-your-sticks-step-step-step-step!"* Stop when they get to the new partner...was everyone together?

9) Try it again, this time if they've got it, keep going around until folks line up with their original partners, then stop there. Incidentally, the facilitator should continue to call out the *"my-sticks-your-sticks-step-step-step-step"* chant and encourage the group to say it as they play it; this helps to keep everyone on the groove.

My sticks, your sticks with partners.

Step, step, step, step...

10) This time, the inside circle will step to the right, and the *outside* circle will also step to the *right*. Yup, to the right; folks may want to say left, but it's got to be the right so the circles move in opposite directions. Players should end up one person down, though some groups move down two (see notes).

11) Have them get set with their partners, then count it off *"One, two, three, four, my-sticks-your-sticks-step-step-step-step!"* There may be a bit of confusion here as some folks move to the left, but that's O.K.; this is where you turn it over to the group to let them communicate and coordinate.

12) Try again, but this time tell the group that they will need to keep the chant going, as you'll simply be holding the Pulse (if possible ask them to choose a person in the group to lead the calls). Let them work on it until they can successfully go around at least twice. Then celebrate!

NOTES

When you introduce the two circle stepping, some groups feel that they need to skip a person in order to move to the right and end up with a new partner. If they all agree, I allow them to do it that way, or work it out however they'd like. Keep in mind that it's not necessary to skip someone for this to work.

Once they've achieved success with the activity, ask the group, "What made this work?" "What part does the Pulse or the rhythm play in making this work?" This activity is a bit tricky for children younger than 4th grade. If you have some background music that has a solid (constant and unchanging) Pulse and a simple beat, you can use that to help with keeping the group on Pulse (Track 4 on the CD is perfect for this).

VARIATIONS

Try playing with the tempo and also throwing in the now famous "Reverse!" Also see *My Sticks, Your Sticks, Dosie Do*, and *My Sticks, Your Sticks Challenge*.

My Sticks, Your Sticks, Dosie Do

GROUP SIZE
Minimum: 8
Maximum: 30 *You'll need an even-numbered group for this activity.*
Challenge Level: 5

TIME
20 minutes

INSTRUMENTS
1 pair of sticks per person
Boomwhackers® Tuned Percussion Tubes can also be used.

FORMATION
Concentric Circles

INSTRUCTIONS

1) This is a great follow up to **My Sticks, Your Sticks**. Once the group successfully performs and understands the basic skills from **My Sticks, Your Sticks**, you can up the challenge here. Remind players to keep sticks in horizontal and vertical positions for safety.

2) As with the previous activity, the inner and outer circles will both step to the right. Practice that sequence again if necessary.

3) Demonstrate with your partner or a participant. The first part of the sequence will remain the same: *my-sticks-your-sticks-step-step-step-step*. Then when you arrive in front of the new partner, the sequence will change a bit. It will be: *my-sticks-your-sticks-switch-switch-switch–switch*. What you'll do here is trade places from outer circle to inner circle in 4 steps. The person on outer circle moves to the inner circle and the person on inner circle moves to the outer circle. They will be switching places instead of stepping to the right. See the diagram on the next page.

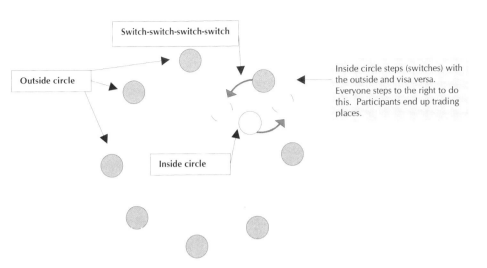

Switch-switch-switch-switch

Outside circle

Inside circle steps (switches) with the outside and visa versa. Everyone steps to the right to do this. Participants end up trading places.

Inside circle

After the switch, all the inside people will end up on the outside circle and vice-versa. They will have just done a basic "dosie do."

Dosie-do...(switch, switch, switch, switch)

4) Get everyone set in front of their partners, and talk them through it so the group can do it together. Start it slow so folks can get the steps.

"One, two, three, four, my-sticks-your-sticks-step-step-step-step (now they are in front of a new partner). *My-sticks-your-sticks-switch-switch-switch–switch* (now they have traded places with that new partner). Everyone together? Practice it slowly until the group has got it.

Remember, it's:
1) *My-sticks-your-sticks-step-step-step-step,*
2) *My-sticks-your-sticks-switch-switch-switch–switch.*

The step and the switch will alternate.

5) If it's being done correctly at this point, the group should notice that they are only trading places with 2 people; their original partner, and the partner to the right. Keep the Pulse for the initial practice, but remember to turn the calls and Pulse over to the group after they have the general idea. Celebrate as they have a smooth flow.

NOTES
For safety, have participants keep the stick positions they started with; that is, if they had them horizontal in the beginning, they will keep them that way no matter where they end up in the circle. The same for the vertical position. As the group succeeds with this phase of the activity, bring in more reflection. Ask again, "What made this work?" "How does the Pulse or the Rhythm support your success?" This activity is as bit tricky for children younger than 4th grade.

VARIATIONS
Tempo changes are also fun with this activity, and can they reverse it? If you have a really skilled group, players on the outside circle will always keep their sticks horizontal, and players on the inside circle always keep their sticks vertical. So, when they switch from inside to outside, they will also need to change stick positions (very challenging!). See **My Sticks, Your Sticks Challenge**, for the final team initiative.

My Sticks, Your Sticks Challenge

GROUP SIZE
Minimum: 8
Maximum: 30 *This is a follow up to* **My Sticks, Your Sticks Dosie Do***; similar group sizes work best.*
Challenge Level: 5

TIME
20 minutes

INSTRUMENTS
1 pair of sticks per person
Boomwhackers® Tuned Percussion Tubes can also be used.

FORMATION
Concentric Circles

INSTRUCTIONS

1) Now that your group has mastered **My Sticks, Your Sticks**, and gotten the swing of the Dosie Do, it's time to let them work on more problem solving skills.

2) As mentioned in the previous activity, if they've done it correctly (given the directions outlined in the activity) the group should only be trading places with 2 people; their original partner, and the partner to the right.

3) Now comes more fun! Ask the group to figure out how to create a flow so that:
    a) *They are still having a switch (i.e. the inner and outer circles are trading places) and,*
    b) *They end up moving around the circles so that they connect with everyone, not just two people.*

4) This *is* in fact possible to do. Your job will simply be to facilitate so that ideas get shared and tried. Let the group come up with the solution. Remind them to use the calls and a Pulse to keep the team together.

NOTES

The answer lies in the group realizing that they must use an alternating left step and right steps, and not just step to the right each time they move. This activity offers some great teamwork and leadership opportunities, and is not recommended for children younger than 5th grade.

VARIATIONS

There is already plenty to deal with here! I'd only add a tempo change (make if faster) for skilled groups.

I go this way, you go that way...hey, I think we got it!

Boomwhackers®
Tuned Percussion Tubes

We're jammin', we're jammin', we're jammin', we're jammin'
We're jammin', we're jammin', we're jammin', we're jammin'
Hope you like jammin', too.
Bob Marley

OVERVIEW

What a cool invention! Boomwhackers® Tuned Percussion Tubes are plastic tubes cut to specific lengths so that they produce tones in a scale. They are lightweight and quite durable. These days you can find them at many toy and music stores. If not, start your search at the source, Whacky Music, Inc. (www.boomwhackers.com) to find local and on-line dealers, or head to International Art and Sound's website at www.shakerman.com.

What I really enjoy about the Boomwhackers® Percussion Tubes is their ability to add musicality to the rhythm experience. Now it's not just about the Pulse, it's also about a melody line. But never fear; it's super easy to play these, and I recommend the C major pentatonically tuned set of the Boomwhackers® as they will sound harmonious no matter which tubes are being played. You can hit the Boomwhackers® Percussion Tubes against just about any surface; hands, or other parts of the body, the floor, chairs, and of course, other Boomwhackers® Tubes.

You can use the Boomwhackers® Tubes for just about all of the games in the sticks section. However, since they come in different lengths (to vary the pitch), try to keep lengths as even as possible in partner activities.

After some hard play, the longer Boomwhackers® Tubes may get a bit bent out of shape. No worries, just place them in a warm room or sunny area for 15 to 20 minutes, then use your hands to smooth them out and round them up again.

For storage, get a duffle bag or if you have an Army Navy surplus store, grab a couple of cotton or canvas pull string laundry bags. This makes your Boomwhackers® easy to store and very portable.

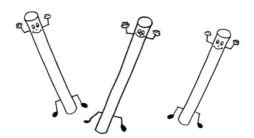

Play a Boom Together

GROUP SIZE
Minimum: 4
Maximum: 30
Challenge Level: 0

TIME
5 to 10 minutes

INSTRUMENTS
One or two Boomwhackers® Tuned Percussion Tubes per person
The facilitator should use an instrument (like a cowbell or jam block) that can be heard above the group.

FORMATION
Large Circle

INSTRUCTIONS
1) Once everyone has their instrument/s, play a Pulse on your bell and have the group hold the Pulse with you for a few moments. Even though the facilitator will hold a Pulse for the duration of the activity, encourage participants to explore their individual rhythms.

2) Play a Pulse and ask participants to play a rhythm that fits with the Pulse, but is *different* than the Pulse (ideally, each person will play their unique rhythm). Remind them that it's totally O.K. to explore; there are no wrong rhythms! Listen to the great improvisational song that happens. Invite them to play yet another rhythm, still fitting with the Pulse but again, different. Call out a 4-count stop.

3) Now begin a Pulse again, and ask players to partner up and create a rhythm together as the main Pulse plays in the background. They can play on each other's Boomwhackers®, or (gently) on each other's legs, arms etc.

4) Have the pairs join up with yet another pair of folks and do the same; creating a rhythm together, different from the Pulse yet fitting within it.

5) Have them join up again so there are at least 6 people in a group all creating a rhythm together. Encourage them to work in connection, that is, their Boomwhackers® hitting their neighbor's Boomwhackers® or legs, etc.

6) Finally, have the entire group working together to create a rhythm. Give them a loud 4-count to bring it to an end.

NOTES

As the subgroups join together, the rhythms may be multi-part grooves and that's fine; the key is to have them interacting with each other as they play. Keep the Pulse so there is always a reference for the tempo and the rhythm.

VARIATIONS

Tempo and volume changes are always good for additional fun. Encourage body movements and chanting to add to the fun of the groove!

Play your "Booms" with your pals!

Peek a Boom

GROUP SIZE
Minimum: 4
Maximum: 30
Challenge Level: 1

TIME
5 to 10 minutes

INSTRUMENTS
1 pair of Boomwhackers® Tuned Percussion Tubes per person
The facilitator will need a pair of Boomwhackers®.

FORMATION
Large Circle *(sitting, facing out)*

INSTRUCTIONS
1) Have each person in the group get one longer and one shorter Boomwhacker®. Ask everyone to form a sitting circle, facing out. You (the facilitator) will be in the center of the circle. This activity is done with eyes closed so the focus can be on listening and feeling the rhythm.

2) Ask participants to keep the longer Boomwhackers® in their right hand, and the shorter in the left. This way, you can utilize the lower and higher notes for more fun and exploration in your call and response.

3) Now, in a call and response fashion, play a simple rhythm with your Boomwhackers®, being clear to accentuate the rhythm so that it is easy to hear the high and low tones used. Start with a slow, simple rhythm, and then get as fast and as complex as the group's skills will allow. Remember, challenge your players, but don't lose them; slow down and simplify if it gets too hard for them to respond.

NOTES
Encourage the participants to keep eyes closed for this activity, as it will really be a lot more fun for them to take on the challenge of listening. Standing behind the group makes it harder for the "peekers" to see which Boomwhackers® you are playing.

VARIATIONS

Utilize tempo changes and give different members of the group an opportunity to come to the center to be the leader.

Concentrating on the response...

1 Boom, 2 Boom, Red Boom, Blue Boom

(Adapted from Arthur Hull)

GROUP SIZE
Minimum: 4
Maximum: 40+
Challenge Level: 2

TIME
5 to 10 minutes

INSTRUMENTS
One or two Boomwhackers® Tuned Percussion Tubes per person
The facilitator will need one of each color Boomwhacker® being used.

FORMATION
Large Circle

INSTRUCTIONS
1) Hand out Boomwhackers® and play a Pulse. Have the group hold the Pulse with you for a few moments to get everyone together. You (the facilitator) will need to stand in as part of the circle so that you don't have your back to anyone; all players should see you clearly. End the Pulse with a 4-count stop.

2) Tell the group that when you start the Pulse again, only those people holding the same color Boomwhacker® should play with you. When you switch colors, those with the new color should play, and those who *were* playing should stop.

So say you began with a red Boomwhacker® Tube; only those folks with red Boomwhackers® should play the Pulse. Now while the red folks are going at it, slowly place the red Boomwhacker® down, switch to a yellow one and play the Pulse. If everyone is watching, the red folks should stop and the yellow folks should kick in with the Pulse. After 30 to 40 seconds or so, reach down, switch colors again, and so on. Make your switches so that you stay in the Pulse.

3) Start with a slow tempo until the group gets the swing of it. You might even do "fake-outs" where you drop a red and immediately pick up a red again! Great for laughs...

NOTES

This is a good activity for focusing a group using visual as well as auditory cues.

VARIATIONS

This gets really fun as you speed up the tempo as well as the speed of your color-to-color transitions. If your group wants to try it, have them close their eyes and switch based solely on the *tone* of the Boomwhacker® they hear. You may want to solo the tones a bit before you do this so they can practice. See ***Colors of the Rhythm*** pg. 71.

Colors of the Rhythm

GROUP SIZE
Minimum: 4
Maximum: 40+
Challenge Level: 3

TIME
5 to 10 minutes

INSTRUMENTS
One or two Boomwhackers® Tuned Percussion Tubes per person
The facilitator will need one of each color Boomwhacker® available.

FORMATION
Large Circle

INSTRUCTIONS
This is a follow up to *1 Boom, 2 Boom, Red Boom, Blue Boom* (pg.69).
Once the group is tuned into your switching the colors during the Pulse, you can do it with rhythms.

1) Assign a different rhythm to each color (they will be able create their own later). Keep the rhythms simple to start; simple patterns work best for novice groups (see the **Rhythm Recipe Ideas** in the Resources section for some ideas). Let each color group have a chance to practice their rhythm.

2) Play a Pulse so everyone has a sense of the tempo, then hold up a color; that group will launch into their rhythm. Let it flow for a bit, then slowly lower that color and switch to another. The first color group should stop as the new color group plays.

3) Be sure to make your color switches at a point in the Pulse so the group-to-group rhythm transitions are smooth. It's O.K. for there to be a bit of overlap from one color to the next; this is natural.

Again, keep it slow until the groups get in the groove.

NOTES

Flowing from rhythm to rhythm is a great way to practice listening and synergizing. If you are new to this, practice it a few times with some friends so you get the feel of it.

VARIATIONS

Let the groups create their own rhythms instead of assigning them. Also, try to have two (or more) colors playing at once...lots of listening needed for that!

A rainbow of Boomwhackers

Maculele (MA-coo-LAY-lay)

GROUP SIZE
Minimum: 10
Maximum: 20 *You'll need an even-numbered group for this activity.*
Challenge Level: 5

TIME
20 to 30 minutes; longer if you get really intricate

INSTRUMENTS
One pair of Boomwhackers® Tuned Percussion Tubes per person
The facilitator will need a pair of Boomwhackers®.

FORMATION
Concentric Circles

INSTRUCTIONS
Maculele is a Brazilian dance that means, "dance of the sticks." It's said to have originated with the slaves who worked in the sugarcane fields and used machetes and cane stalks to create the dance. Other stories claim that it has similar roots as Capoeira; a martial art disguised as a dance.

We'll modify the traditional Maculele moves for our purposes here.

1) Hand out Boomwhackers® and have your group form two circle (concentric) as if setting up for **My Sticks, Your Sticks**. The first thing to do is get the group going with a round of **My Sticks, Your Sticks**, so they get in the groove.

2) Next, do a round of **My Sticks, Your Sticks Dosie Do** to warm up for Maculele. For the Maculele moves I've described here, I'll *always* keep the movements to the right. You can modify to add left movements with your group as they get more comfortable and want that challenge.

3) Now we'll add some Maculele moves. Keep a slow Pulse until they get the hang of it. The first sequence (and chant) will be: *my-sticks-your-sticks-step-step-step-step*, then *my-sticks-floor-sticks-turn-a-round-and-your-sticks*. On *floor-sticks,* simply bend down to hit the Boomwhackers® twice on the floor (following the cadence of the chant).

On *turn-a-round-and*, individuals will spin 360 in place to the right, hitting the Boomwhackers® together 3 times to follow the cadence of the chant, then as they face their partner again, it's *your-sticks* (hitting partner's Boomwhackers® two times as usual). Try this a few times before moving on.

4) The next sequence (and chant) goes like this: *right-sticks-left-sticks-sticks-up-high-spin-sticks*. Wow! O.K., let's break it down.

On *right-sticks* partners hit their right hand Boomwhackers® twice (right hand to right hand).

Then on *left-sticks* they hit their left hand Boomwhackers® twice (left hand to left hand).

On *sticks-up-high*, players hold both Boomwhackers® up above their heads and hit their own Boomwhackers® together 3 times (on each syllable).

Then on *spin* it's a super quick 360 turn in place so they can hit their own Boomwhackers® together (up high) on the Pulse for the final *sticks*. Try that a few times so the group gets the sequence.

5) Here's a review of the sequences so far. Remind the players to chant as they move; this really helps!
1)   *My-sticks-your-sticks-step-step-step-step*
2)   *My-sticks-floor-sticks-turn-a-round-and-your-sticks*
3)   *Right-sticks-left-sticks-sticks-up-high-spin-sticks*

At this point (after sequence 3) partners should be facing each other in the same circles in which they began.

6) Now we'll do the dosie do: *my-sticks-your-sticks-switch-switch-switch-switch* (partners trade spots moving to the right).

And next: *right-left-ground-ground-ground-ground, right-left-step-step-step-step*.

So, this will be right hand to right hand one hit, then left to left one hit, then 4 hits on the ground.

Then right hand to right hand one hit, then left to left one hit, then 4 steps to the right (hitting one's own Boomwhackers®) to line up with a new partner. The "new" partner should be the partner with whom the whole activity began. *Celebrate!*

7) The whole sequence starts again from here. Here's the full dance:
   1) *My-sticks-your-sticks-step-step-step-step*
   2) *My-sticks-floor-sticks-turn-a-round-and-your-sticks*
   3) *Right-sticks-left-sticks-sticks-up-high-spin-sticks*
   4) *My-sticks-your-sticks-switch-switch-switch-switch*

Right-left-ground-ground-ground-ground, right-left-step-step-step-step.

NOTES

The choreography here is actually easier than it appears. The key is to stay with the Pulse (slow at first), and explore the movement.

VARIATIONS

You can add as many interesting moves as you and your group can create and choreograph. Increasing the tempo increases the fun. Remember, you can improvise and get very creative with the movements, including adding movements right **and** left if your group wants to experiment...enjoy!

Right-sticks...

Hear that?

Sound Shapes ®

"No man, however civilized, can listen for very long to African drumming, or Indian singing, or Welsh hymn singing, and retain intact his critical and self-conscious personality."

Aldous huxley

OVERVIEW

Of the coolest new drum variations to hit the market, Sound Shapes®
get top billing in my book. These are specially designed frame drums,
created by the innovative folks at Remo USA (www.remo.com). Sound
Shapes® consist of a strong plastic drumhead material, sandwiched
between layers of Remo's sturdy Acousticon® drum shell material. You
can get them in a variety of shapes and colors and they all sound
fantastic.

In the circular Sound Shapes® pack you get six drums ranging from 6"
to 16" in diameter and colors blue, purple, black, yellow, green, or red.
The other shapes include a 9" triangle, a 6.5x9" rectangle, a 9x9"
square, a 9" circle, and a 9" wide half-circle. All the sets come with
strong plastic beaters. Even though you can use regular drumsticks on
the Sound Shapes®, I highly recommend using the included plastic
beaters; they will sound just as good, and lessen the wear and tear on
your Sound Shapes®.

The multi-shapes sound just as good as the circles and have neat
applications for younger children. I prefer the circular Sound Shapes®
sets however, as they are easier to store and are a great buy. The
activities in this section assume you are using the circular shapes, but
the other shapes will work just as well.

If you get more than one set of the circle shapes, you can nest them
together to create layers for storage. This way you can get up to 30
drums in a stack that's only 12 inches tall; very compact for that many
drums. You can pick up an inexpensive backpack (at a local a Ross, TJ
Max, or Target), and you'll have a great way to store and travel these
cool instruments. If you get a large selection of Sound Shapes®,
another small stuff sack will hold the beaters.

Math Pulse

GROUP SIZE
Minimum: 2
Maximum: 40+ This is a great activity for elementary school aged children (2nd to 5th grade).
Challenge Level: 1

TIME
5 minutes

INSTRUMENTS
One Sound Shape® and beater per participant
This activity also works well with other instruments.
The facilitator should use an instrument (like a cowbell or jam block) that can be heard above the group.

FORMATION
Large Circle or Conglomerate

INSTRUCTIONS
1) Start out playing a Pulse and invite the group to join in so they are all in sync; use a 4-count stop to end the Pulse after 30 seconds or so ("One-two-three-four-STOP!").

2) Tell the group that when you begin the Pulse again, they need to play it very softly. Try it, and then end with another 4-count stop.

3) Now tell the group that while they play the Pulse, you are going to call out numbers. Their job is to play that many hits really loud (and double time to the Pulse) and go right back to the Pulse. Give a demonstration first.

4) Play a soft Pulse then say, "3-ready-play!" Your "3-ready-play!" should be chanted on the Pulse. Hit 3 beats really loud and then go right back to the soft Pulse. Do another demonstration if necessary. If you are working with younger children, remind them not to play the loud hits until you say "ready, play!" This will give them a cue and keep the group together, especially if you keep your chant on the Pulse.

5) Start the group with a soft Pulse again and practice with a few small numbers, increasing the number of hits as the group gets the hang of it.

6) Once they understand how this works, tell them to listen even more carefully, as you are now going to use math problems instead of actual numbers. It might help to add a moment to think as part of the chant. As they play a soft Pulse, you'll say *"2-plus-3-and-think-ready-play!"* If they can do the math in their head, they should play 5 hits then go back to the soft Pulse. Try another; *"4-plus-4-and-think-ready-play!"*

7) Do a few rounds with simple equations, advancing with the groups ability. Use a 4-count stop to end.

NOTES

This is a "math and music" activity that's great for elementary aged children, but (with or without the math facts) can be fun for groups of all ages. Listening and playing the hits tunes the group to each other and the Pulse. From time to time, you may need to get the group back on a Pulse, so encourage them to listen for it as they play and keep it strong with your instrument.

VARIATIONS

Use other math skills (subtraction, multiplication, division) if you have a more advanced or appropriate group. You may want to create flashcards to give you cues for the right equations to use with each group.

Incidentally, this is a great way for teachers to practice class vocabulary words; call out the word and have them chant the spelling in beat with the Pulse.

Shape Up!

GROUP SIZE

Minimum: 4
Maximum: 20 You'll need an even number of participants for this activity.
Challenge Level: 1

TIME

10 minutes

INSTRUMENTS

One Sound Shape® and beater per participant
The facilitator should use an instrument (like a cowbell or jam block) that can be heard above the group.

FORMATION

Parallel Lines

INSTRUCTIONS

1) Once all participants have an instrument, have them line up in two single file lines facing each other. Once set, each person should be facing a partner.

2) Instrument positioning is key here. Each partner will hold their Sound Shape® in their left hand and the beater in the right. The Sound Shape® should be held waist high with the playing surface (the head) facing up. Participants should be able to hit their own drums (in their left hand) then hit their partner's drums across the line.

3) Once they've all lined up to do this, invite players to hold a Pulse by hitting their shape twice, and their partner's shape twice alternatively. You can add the vocal chant (see **My sticks, Your sticks**) only here it will be "my-shape-your-shape."

4) Keep it slow then increase the tempo of the Pulse until you reach the maximum for the group. Bring the tempo down slowly, and then call a 4-count stop *("One-two-three-four-STOP!")*.

5) For the next round of play, have participants hit the top of their shape and the underside of their partner's shape; this adds a different focus.

As the players get more comfortable, you can up the challenge with some creative combinations.
Try these with your group:

    a) The underside of both shapes: The chant is, **"Un-der-un-der"** *(Two hits on their own shape, then two hits on their partner's shapes.)*

    b) The underside of their shape and the top of their partner's shape: The chant is, **"Un-der-top."** *(Two hits on their own shape then one hit on their partner's shape.)*

    c) The underside of both shapes and top of their partner's shape: The chant is, **"Un-der-un-der-top."** *(Two hits on their own shape then two hits on their partner's shape, then a hit on either theirs OR their partner's shape.)*

    d) The top of both shapes and the underside of their partner's shape: The chant is, **"Top-top-top-top-un-der."** *(Two hits on their own shape then two hits on their partner's shape, then a hit on either theirs OR their partner's shape.)*

6) These examples give you the basics of what's possible. Feel free to experiment; I highly recommend trying some at home before you facilitate. You can also let members of the group experiment with creating combinations for fun. End each combination groove with a good ol' 4-count stop.

NOTES
As the group plays, do they focus so much on where they are playing that they forget to hold the drums for their partners? This a great process question.

VARIATIONS
Have the whole group, or just partners depending on the group's abilities, walk around the room *(as a unit)* to the beat of the Pulse while they play. Can they keep the rhythm and the partner connection while they move? It's a fun challenge! Also see the next activity **Soup's On** (pg. 85).

Size Em' Up

GROUP SIZE
Minimum: 6
Maximum: 40 +
Challenge Level: 1

TIME
10 minutes

INSTRUMENTS
One Sound Shape® and beater per participant
The facilitator will need one of each Sound Shape® size in the collection.

FORMATION
Large Circle

INSTRUCTIONS
This activity is similar to **Colors of the Rhythm** (pg. 71).

1) Hand out shapes and invite the group to sit or stand in a circle. Stand where the entire group can easily see you.

2) Explain that you will begin with a Pulse, and the Pulse should only be played by those people holding the same size Sound Shape® as you play. When you switch sizes, those with the new size should play, and those who *were* playing should stop.

3) Begin a Pulse with the largest shape; only those folks with large shapes should play the Pulse with you. Now while the large shape folks are playing, slowly switch to the smallest shape and play the Pulse. The folks with the smallest shape should now play, and the large shape folks will stop.

4) Move through all the sizes, keeping the Pulse alive and allowing the players to get the hang of the switch; try to keep your switches with the Pulse (start off slowly).

5) Keep the Pulse going with the last shape you held up (keep holding it up high). Let that group of shape sizes hold the Pulse, while you set down your beater, and pick up another size shape (the group will hold the *Pulse*). Now, two different sizes should be playing. As players get the hang of it, you can begin to increase the speed of the Pulse, as well as the speed of your size switching and adding.

6) Bring it to a close with a 4-count stop, and if your group is into it, try a few of the variations below.

NOTES

Similar to **Color the Pulse**, this gets a group to focus and listen. It also highlights the various voices in the Sound Shape® ensemble.

VARIATIONS

Try giving the various shape sizes different rhythms (see **Colors of the Rhythm**, pg. 71) and by switching or adding shapes, you can play with the sound of the grooves. Try standing behind the group and then switch shape sizes; their only cue will be auditory. Can they do it?

Play 'em small, then play 'em big....

Soup's on

GROUP SIZE
Minimum: 2
Maximum: 20 *You'll need an even number of participants for this activity.*
Challenge Level: 2

TIME
10 minutes

INSTRUMENTS
One Sound Shape® and beater per participant
The facilitator should use an instrument (like a cowbell) that can be heard above the group.

FORMATION
Parallel Lines

INSTRUCTIONS
1) Arrange participants as in **Shape Up!** (pg. 81).

2) Remember that instrument positioning is important. Have the group play a *"my-shape-your-shape"* groove to get aligned.

3) Choose a recipe from the **Rhythm Recipes** list on page 131. First, have the entire group play each line of the recipe together. Group members will typically play all parts on the tops of the shapes.

4) Next have partner pairs play various "ingredients" from the recipe, and invite them to switch their playing so they hit the undersides as well the tops of the shapes.

5) After some practice, assign specific pairs to play ingredients from the recipe. Depending on their comfort, encourage them to keep playing the tops and undersides of the shapes. Pair by pair, you will be constructing a groove that incorporates all the ingredients; you may need to keep the Pulse strong and loud so all pairs can use it to keep themselves in the groove.

Once you get the whole group rockin' let the rhythm flow until just before the rhythm starts to fall apart (you'll be able to tell as the sound moves from a unified groove to chaotic sound), then call a 4-count stop and bring it to an end. *Celebrate!*

NOTES

Encourage the group to listen for the interplay between the various recipe lines; this is the magic of what's called "polyrhythm," and is a key element to many traditional rhythms from around the world. Polyrhythm also provides another opportunity for the group to listen and synergize.

VARIATIONS

Feel free to use any rhythm grooves (you can create them in the moment!), and invite the group to create grooves as well. Vary tempos and also add moving around the room. Movements increase the fun factor as well as the challenge.

Bowl a' Beats

GROUP SIZE
Minimum: 8
Maximum: 30 *You'll need an even number of participants for this activity.*
Challenge Level: 4

TIME
10 minutes

INSTRUMENTS
One Sound Shape® and beater per participant
The facilitator should use an instrument (like a cowbell or jam block) that can be heard above the group.

FORMATION
Concentric Circles

INSTRUCTIONS

1) Divide your group in two and form concentric circles. Each player should have a partner, one standing on the inside circle, the other standing in the outside circle.

Participants will hold their Sound Shapes® as in **Shape Up!** (pg. 81). Each partner will hold their Sound Shape® in their left hand and the beater in the right. The Sound Shape® should be held waist high with the playing surface (the head) facing up. Participants should be able to hit their own drums (in their left hand) then hit their partner's drums in the other circle.

2) Align partners, set up instrument positioning, and have the group play a "my-shape-your-shape" groove to get set. End with a 4-count stop.

3) If you already have an even-numbered group, you (the facilitator) should get into the middle of the inner circle, the "center of the bowl." From the center, play a few rounds of call-and-response rhythms *(see page 43)* on your cowbell or jam block to focus the group.

If you are going to be a player in a circle, you should use a small Sound Shape® as those create a note that can more easily be heard above the rest of the group; use your Sound Shape® for the call and response rhythms. Make up the rhythms, use your favorites, or choose from the recipes list (pg. 131).

5) It's time to rotate! Start the entire group playing their Sound Shapes® and chanting, *"my-shape-your-shape."* When you give the signal, the inside circle will step to the right, and the outside circle will step to the left while chanting *"my-shape-your-shape."*

Both circles will be rotating in the same direction (for now) so that players stay with the same partner. Encourage them to keep the chant going as they move. Do a full rotation, then call 4-count stop. Rotate in the other direction so your group can get a more practice. Use a few of the variations below or move on to the next activity to up the challenge.

NOTES

Moving while playing, calls on each participant's ability to multi-task using auditory and kinesthetic cues.

VARIATIONS

Feel free to use rhythm grooves you create, and invite the group to create grooves and play the tops and undersides of Sound Shapes®. Vary tempos and add directional movement (i.e., the whole group moving from point A to B around the room *while* the rotation is happening)...oh, yeah!

Beat Vortex

GROUP SIZE
Minimum: 2
Maximum: 30 *You'll need an even number of participants for this activity.*
Challenge Level: 5

TIME
15 minutes

INSTRUMENTS
One Sound Shape® and beater per participant
The facilitator should use an instrument (like a cowbell or jam block) that can be heard above the group.

FORMATION
Concentric Circles

INSTRUCTIONS
1) This is a follow up activity to ***Bowl a' Beats*** (pg 87)**;** participants will be arranged in concentric circles, facing a partner.

2) In ***Bowl a' Beats*** the inner and outer circles moved in the same direction while the participants kept a rhythm. We'll increase the challenge here; now participants need to work together following 3 rules:

    a) *Keep a Pulse or rhythm going;*

    b) *Play their shape **as well as** the shape of other people who are in a **different** circle than they are; and,*

    c) *Have the circles move in **opposite** directions (the inner circle steps to the right, and the outer circle **also** steps to the right).*

3) Provide the instructions to the group, and clarify as needed. Step back and let the group process unfold. Facilitate as necessary to keep them on track. Encourage them to actually try some ideas. Groups sometimes have a tendency to talk about ideas without jumping in to explore and gather real-time (instead of hypothetical) data; this is a great point for a debrief discussion. Groups that have played ***My Sticks, Your Sticks*** (pg. 53) should have some ideas of how to start. You (the facilitator) will play a Pulse, or you can use the Pulse Tracks on the CD.

4) Remind the group to use vocal chants (i.e.: *my-shape-your-shape-step-step-step* etc.) as part of their process, as it will help the group stay aligned.

NOTES

There are many ways the group can succeed at the task and these range from simple to relatively complex (see *My Sticks, Your Sticks Challenge* pg. 61). The key in succeeding is for the group to use the Pulse as the foundation, and to once again utilize what I refer to as the *4 C's*: Communication, Cooperation, Creativity, and Compassion.

VARIATIONS

If the group is up for it, invite them to accomplish the task with a rhythm more complex than just a Pulse, and as always, throw in the "Reverse!" command and tempo changes. For a really advanced group, have them make concentric squares or triangles instead of circles.

walk, play...and keep the groove!

Top Ten Challenge (Learned from my friend Anugrah)

GROUP SIZE
Minimum: 2
Maximum: 30
Challenge Level: 5 (Not recommended for participants younger than 5th grade)

TIME
10 minutes

INSTRUMENTS
One Sound Shape® and beater per participant; other types of instruments can be used
The facilitator will need a jam block or cow bell to keep the Pulse.

FORMATION
Parallel Lines (neighbors should stand shoulder to shoulder)

INSTRUCTIONS
1) Hand out shapes and have the group stand in parallel lines (shoulder to shoulder) with the lines facing each other. If you have an even group, each person will have a partner across the line from them, but even groups are not necessary for the activity.

2) One line will play a call, and the other line will respond, but there is a specific pattern. You will play a slow Pulse (at first) to keep the groups in sync.

3) The pattern goes like this. *Line A* plays 1 hit on the pulse, and then *Line B* responds with 9 hits. Then *Line A* plays 2 hits on the Pulse, and *Line B* responds with 8 hits. What's happening here is that *Line A* is counting up from 1 to 9, and *Line B* is counting down from 9 to 1; the total of all beats played by both groups is always 10.

The rules are: **1)** *Hits must stay on the Pulse.*
2) *Players can only play their instrument (no talking) during play.*
3) *If either line makes a mistake, both lines should start again from the top.*

The pattern sounds like this:

Line A	Line B
Hit (1)	Hit-hit-hit-hit-hit-hit-hit-hit-hit (9)
Hit-hit (2)	Hit-hit-hit-hit-hit-hit-hit-hit (8)
Hit-hit-hit (3)	Hit-hit-hit-hit-hit-hit-hit (7)
Hit-hit-hit-hit (4)	Hit-hit-hit-hit-hit-hit (6)
And so on…	

4) Begin a nice slow Pulse and then give Line A, a 4-count to begin say, *"One-two-three-four-play!"* Line A begins on the beat **after** *"Play!"* Remember to start this with a really slow Pulse; it's trickier than it seems. End when the group's energy wanes, or they have gotten all the way through the pattern…and celebrate!

NOTES

The game sounds easy, but actually requires that the participants work very closely with each other. They must listen to the Pulse to stay in sync, *and* focus on the pattern. This is an excellent team focusing activity.

VARIATIONS

Speed up the Pulse once the group gain some skill. How quickly can they do this without messing up? Also, have them count back to 9 once they've reached the end of the first pattern set (*Line A* starts at 9 and *Line B* starts at 1 etc.).

Multi-Instrument Activities

"Music and rhythm find their way into the secret places of the soul."
Plato

OVERVIEW

These are games that utilize your entire ensemble of instruments. Though they can be done with a homogenous collection, the more instruments you add, the more diverse and interesting the sound.

Let the ensemble rock!

Rhythm Machine

GROUP SIZE
Minimum: 4
Maximum: 30
Challenge Level: 1

TIME
10 minutes.

INSTRUMENTS
This works well with just about any instrument, one per participant. *The facilitator should use an instrument (like a cowbell) that can be heard above the group.*

FORMATION
Large Circle

INSTRUCTIONS

1) The facilitator plays a Pulse, and invites a brave member of the group to step into the middle of the circle and start a relatively simple rhythm. Now ask another member of the group to physically connect with the first person in the circle (they may link arms or stand back to back with heels touching). The new person will play a different rhythm that fits with the first. You'll now have two people connected, and two rhythms playing (plus your Pulse).

2) Invite a third person out, and so on until you have the whole group (or as many people as possible) connected and rockin' out.

3) Cheer them on and give a loud 4-count to end, "One-two-three-four-stop!"

NOTES
As more folks join the rhythm, you'll need to keep the Pulse steady, or ask those still in the circle to hold the Pulse with you. Encourage each new person to listen to the rhythms so they can add to the rhythm machine without making it crash.

Also, encourage them to physically connect with each other in ways that are creative yet respectful (i.e. ways that do not disrupt another player's rhythm or movements).

VARIATIONS

You can have the participants make a movement as well as a rhythm to which others add their own corresponding movements and rhythms...the result has a really great effect! You can also ask the last player who joined the "rhythm machine," to step back to the circle and join the Pulse. Then continue reversing the order of participants until the last player (who was the first) comes back to the original circle. Now everyone is playing the Pulse again and you can end with a 4-count stop.

Jam baby!

Small Group Groove

GROUP SIZE
Minimum: 8
Maximum: 40
Challenge Level: 2

TIME
30 minutes

INSTRUMENTS
Use all the instruments you have, one or two per participant depending on group size and the size of your instrument collection.

FORMATION
Small Groups

INSTRUCTIONS
1) Divide the large group into small groups of 3 to 6 people depending on the size of the large group.

2) Ask each member of a smaller group to get an instrument, and ask them to mix the instruments in the small groups so they have as varied a collection as possible.

3) Instruct each group to create a groove. The groove should have a formal beginning, instrument solos during the groove, and a formal end. They will have 10 minutes to practice, and then each group will perform their rhythm. Remind each group to have a Pulse keeper; the Pulse keeper can change to another rhythm if they'd like, once the groove gets going.

4) Give the groups a two or three minutes warning so they can finalize their performances. Ask for a volunteer group to start the show, and loudly celebrate each groups presentation!

NOTES

This is another great activity for utilizing your instrument collection. It gives participants a chance to create their own rhythm and work together for a common groove (goal). It also allows all the (metaphoric) voices within the subgroups a chance to shine. Mill around during the groove creation time to give suggestions and offer encouragement.

VARIATIONS

Require the groups to add body movements and vocalizations to the grooves (if you have willing participants); this adds another element of fun to the activity.

Groovin' together...

Rhythm Stories

GROUP SIZE
Minimum: 8
Maximum: 40
Challenge Level: 2

TIME
30 minutes

INSTRUMENTS
This works well with just about any instrument, one or two per participant depending on group size and the size of your instrument collection.

FORMATION
Small Groups

INSTRUCTIONS
1) Divide the large group into smaller groups of 3 to 6 people depending on the size of the large group.

2) Invite each member of a smaller group to get an instrument (or two), and encourage them to vary the instruments in the small groups so they have an eclectic mix.

3) Ask each group to create a story, and use their instruments in telling the story; they can use words, and must also use their instruments to accentuate the story. Each group will have 10 minutes to create and practice their story, then they'll each share with the whole group. Groups can choose to work with an existing story (e.g. a well known folk tale or nursery rhyme, etc.), but encourage them to make one up from scratch, and to be creative with using the instruments.

4) Let participants know when they have a minute or so of practice time left so they can finalize the story and presentation. Bring the groups back together and ask for a volunteer group to start the show. Cheer and celebrate each group as they present!

NOTES

This is a great activity for using all the instruments you have and gives participants a chance to "own the sounds" by experimenting with how they play the instruments. Walk around to different groups to offer creative support during their story creation process. I have found this activity to work best with participants from 4th grade on up.

VARIATIONS

If the groups are willing, have them tell the stories using only instruments, and see if the other groups can translate the general ideas of the stories to words. See **Rhythm Conversations** on page 101.

Tellin' tales with rhythm.

Rhythm Conversations

GROUP SIZE
Minimum: 4
Maximum: 40
Challenge Level: 3

TIME
15 minutes; longer if the group gets into it

INSTRUMENTS
This works well with just about any instrument, one or two per participant depending on group size and the size of your collection.

FORMATION
Small Groups

INSTRUCTIONS
1) Divide the large group into smaller groups of 2 to 3 people.

2) Ask each group to make up a conversation or the scenario for a conversation. For example, scenarios could be a person chatting to a neighbor over the fence, a person talking with a grocery line clerk, or people in line at a bank. Have them brainstorm fun situations in their small groups (or pairs).

3) Their task will be to use the instruments to have the conversations in front of the large group. The large group's task will be to figure out what scenario is being played out, and if possible, what's being said. *No actual verbal communication can be used; only the instruments can make the sounds.*

4) After a conversation has been presented let each of the observing small groups have a minute to discuss what they interpreted, then come back and share what they believe the conversation was about. The closest interpretation wins a hearty round of applause.

NOTES

This is a great improvisation oriented activity. Use it with groups that have a lot of playful energy and are willing to explore. I have found that this activity works best with participants from 4th grade on up.

VARIATIONS

If the groups need some support, you could let them add charades movements to give hints to the audience.

Speaking through the groove...

Sound Wave (Learned from Chris Cavert)

GROUP SIZE
Minimum: 4
Maximum: 30
Challenge Level: 3 (Not recommended for participants younger than 5th grade)

TIME
15 to 30 minutes depending on group size and ability

INSTRUMENTS
This works well with just about any instrument, one per participant. If you have a stopwatch, this will add to the fun.

FORMATION
Large Circle

INSTRUCTIONS
The task here is to pass a sound around the group without missing a beat. Have the group stand in a large circle with their instrument.

1) First the group must establish an order of sound moving throughout the circle. Choose someone to start, and ask them to "pass the sound." This means, they'll play one hit on their instrument as if directing the sound to another person across the circle (like they are "passing" the sound). The receiver then does the same, and directs a hit across the circle to another person. Continue with each player receiving a hit and passing a hit. The person receiving the last hit "sends" it back to the first person.

2) Participants **must** remember the person to whom they passed the sound (so they can keep the same order). Each person recives and passes the sound **once**.

3) Now you can throw in the rules.
   1) No two participants can make a sound at the same time.
   2) The sound must travel around in the same order they established.

3) *Every participant must make a sound. (That is, if there are 15 people in the circle, you should hear 15 sounds.)*

4) Give them some time to practice getting the sounds passed around. Once they have it, provide a slow Pulse, and see if they can pass the sound around without missing a beat, keeping each person in the order they established.

5) Now up the challenge. Tell them their task is to get the sound passed around the circle as fast as possible, while adhering to the 3 rules. Let them know you would be happy to play a Pulse for them if they'd like it (if you can do that while you time them).

It may take a few rounds, but eventually someone in the group will figure out that they can still maintain the order by moving folks around so that they are standing in the right sequence (i.e. the first person standing next to the second person and so on instead of random placement around the circle). This does not violate any of the rules, and gives them a new advantage.

If they have not figured this out, challenge them by explaining that it *really is* possible to pass the sound in a very short amount of time (say 3 to 5 seconds depending on group size). This usually encourages more "out of the box" thinking, since they now know the task is possible.

NOTES

Don't necessarily give away the answer; if they do not get it, encourage them to keep thinking or talking about it as you move on to other activities. This way, the group owns the problem solving process. Also ask them how the Pulse may support the process. For those who have played a game called "Warp Speed" (Karl Rhonke), ask them to remain mute (at least for a little while) so the rest of the group can discover the solution, which is similar.

VARIATIONS

If each person in the group has a different sounding instrument, have them try this with their eyes closed. If you have no instruments, this will work with participants making a predetermined vocal sound or a clap; just make sure the sound is loud enough for each person to hear it.

Follow the Leader (Learned from Gabriela Masala)

GROUP SIZE
Minimum: 4
Maximum: 20
Challenge Level: 4

TIME
15 to 30 minutes depending on group size and ability
This may not work well with younger participants.

INSTRUMENTS
This works well with just about any instrument, one per participant.

FORMATION
Small Groups

INSTRUCTIONS
1) Break your large group into subgroups of 4 people each. If you are unable to divide your group into 4's, extra folks can rotate in and out of groups.

2) Have each person in the small group stand so they are at each end of an invisible plus sign (+).

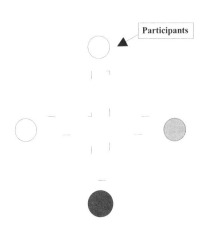

Participants

3) Ask all four people to face the same direction. The person at the head of the plus sign (the person with their back to the other 3 people) is the leader. This person plays a rhythm and does a continuous body movement; the other three people copy the rhythm and the movement.

4) When the lead person makes a quarter turn to the right (so that a new person is at the head of the plus sign) the new person takes over, creating a new rhythm and movement for the other three people to imitate. *The turns and transitions should be smooth and slow enough for the shift in leadership to be easy.*

5) This goes on around the "plus sign" to the right (clockwise) until it comes back to the original leader. The key is to be spontaneous, yet predictable enough for the group to stay in sync; thus, the wonderful challenge of the activity.

6) Once groups have had 5 to 10 minutes to practice, have each group share for the other small groups. Cheer them on as they play!

NOTES

Encourage the groups to improvise as they explore rhythms and movements; there is a lot of creativity available here. This activity encourages individuals to focus, connect, and support each other. Their follow-the-leader sequences are really fun to hear and beautiful to watch.

VARIATIONS

Switch leaders in different directions (randomly) instead of one direction around the "plus sign;" leadership could flow to the right, and back to the left, and so on instead of just clockwise.

If I Play...

GROUP SIZE
Minimum: 4
Maximum: 30
Challenge Level: 5

TIME
10 minutes.

INSTRUMENTS
This works well with just about any instrument, one per participant. *The facilitator should use an instrument (like a cowbell or jam block) that can be heard above the group.*

FORMATION
Large Circle or Conglomerate

INSTRUCTIONS
1) This is a call and response game, so a one-minute round of **Call and Response** (pg. 43) will get the group ready. Remember that the *call* is the part you play; the *response* is the part the group plays as an echo to the call.

2) Tell the group "We will keep doing call and response, with you echoing back what I play. BUT if I play 3 beats, you all respond with one LOUD beat, then wait for the next call. Practice the 3 beats/one loud beat call and response pattern with the group a few times so they get it.

3) Now go back to "regular" call and response, inserting the 3 beat call between your other call and response patterns.

NOTES
This is another spin on a group cohesion exercise. The point is to keep the group listening, focusing, and playing together, while adding an element of surprise. Put the 3 beat call in when they least expect it!

VARIATIONS

There are limitless variations to this activity. You can choose just about any call and any response to that call (see **Rhythm Recipes** on pg. 131 for some ideas). Calls and responses can also integrate vocal chants as well as beats on instruments. For example if I am playing on a cow bell a simple call and response with a vocal might be:

CALL: *Clang-clang-clang-"HEY!"*
RESPONSE: *Beat-"HUH!"-beat -"HUH!"-beat -"HUH!"-"HUH!"*

"Beat" represents the response hits the group plays in unison on their various instruments. Make your call and response creations fun for the group, but aligned with the group's skill level; you don't want to confuse them.

You can also use basic math for call and response. For example, tell your group that you will play a call, and their response must add with your call to total 8. It might sound like this (if the call is on a cowbell):

CALL: *Clang-clang-clang-clang (4 hits)*
RESPONSE: *Clang-clang-clang-clang (4 hits)*
The call and the response add up to 8.

CALL: *Clang-clang (2 hits)*
RESPONSE: *Clang-clang-clang-clang-clang-clang (6 hits)*
The call and the response add up to 8.

CALL: *Clang-clang-clang (3 hits)*
RESPONSE: *Clang-clang-clang-clang-clang (5 hits)*
The call and the response add up to 8.

You get the idea...again, keep the math skills appropriate to the level of the group.

CD Tracks

"Remember, it's all about the GROOVE! The groove is Queen."
Kenya Masala

This section includes song activities that can be done with tracks 5 and 6 on the CD. Tracks 5 and 6 are vocal versions of songs, and tracks 7 and 8 are instrumental versions.

The tracks with vocals let you play the movement games or sing along to learn the song. The instrumental versions are for general jamming along or leading your own song. The intent is for you to learn the song so that you can lead it in "call and response" fashion. Once you've learned the song and the movements, add your own flair.

The rhythms used for both the vocal and instrumental versions of the songs are simply accompaniments; they are just rhythm ideas for you to use. Feel free to explore and make up your own accompaniment grooves once you've learned the melodies of the songs.

Tracks 1 through 3 on the CD are Pulse tracks to assist in keeping a Pulse with any activity in the book. Track 4 is a simple jam track...play along and create your own groove to add to the rhythm!

Let's all play!

CD Tracks one, Two, Three: Pulse Tracks

GROUP SIZE
Minimum: N/A
Maximum: N/A
Challenge Level: 0

TIME
2 minutes per tempo *(CD Track Length)*

INSTRUMENTS
This works well with any instrument (one per participant), or just clapping hands.

FORMATION
All (Pulse Tracks can be used along with any formation)

INSTRUCTIONS
Theses tracks are simply for use as a Pulse. Use them if you are in an activity, and not able to play a constant Pulse for your group. You can also use the tracks as background for chanting or playing around with *Rhythm Recipe Ideas* on page 131.

NOTES
Each Pulse track lasts for 2 minutes; subsequent tracks increase in tempo by about 10 beats per minute.

VARIATIONS
Again, use the Pulses in whatever way you feel inspired; they are simply support tools.

CD Track four:Jam Track

GROUP SIZE
Minimum: 1
Maximum: 40+
Challenge Level: 0

TIME
5 minutes *(CD Track Length)*

INSTRUMENTS
This works well with just about any instrument (one per participant), or just clapping hands. *Remember that hands get tired after about 5 minutes of continuous clapping.*

FORMATION
Conglomerate or Large Circle (Standing or Sitting)

INSTRUCTIONS
This track is simply for playing along. The groove builds in stages to give you an idea of polyrhythmic layering. With the Jam Track playing, invite players join into the groove. Then have everyone play softly while inviting one player at a time to play a solo while the rest of the group cheers them on. Solos are opportunities for a player to do their own thing within the context of the rhythm. Solos let the group hear the unique contribution each player brings to the circle. They can be whatever comes to mind, even if it's just one note! If you bring solos into the rhythm jam, be sure to celebrate each person's solo during and after.

Solos can be passed around the group from player to player. When one player finishes their solo, they can pass it with a **very clear** hand gesture to their neighbor or someone across the circle if they are in circle formation. I recommend the facilitator starting the solo play so the "solo passing gesture" can be clearly shown at the beginning of solo play.

ou can use the Jam Track for your solo practice sessions, or as a good
ackground rhythm for a raucous jam.

NOTES

he instruments played on the Jam Track are traditional percussion instru-
ents from West Africa: the djembe, the dun-duns, shakers, and iron bells.
eel free to use any instruments you have to play along.

VARIATIONS

Vhatever you feel inspired to do! This one is purely for enjoyment and play.

CD Track Five: Bambale (Bam-ba-Lay)

GROUP SIZE
Minimum: 8
Maximum: 40+
Challenge Level: 1

TIME
5 minutes *(CD Track Length)*

INSTRUMENTS
This works well with just about any instrument (one per participant), or just clapping hands.

FORMATION
Large Circle

INSTRUCTIONS

1) Gather the group in one large circle; the facilitator stands in the middle of the circle, with their instrument of choice.

2) Teach the group the call and response words to the chorus. Once they have it down, begin a Pulse and play it until the entire group is together. Now try doing the call and response part of the song to the Pulse. You might start out by just keeping the pulse with hand claps before using instruments, as playing and singing can be somewhat challenging at first.

3) Once the group gets the song with the Pulse, it's time to add some steps. Have everyone make a quarter turn to the LEFT. The group should now be standing so each person is looking at the back of the person in front of them (all the way around the circle).

4) When **you** call, the group will walk forward (the circle will rotate clockwise). When **they respond**, the group will walk backwards (the circle will rotate counter-clockwise). If you count, it will be 4 steps forwards, and 4 steps back. It's best just to feel it instead of counting as that can be confusing.

5) On the A-LAY part of the song, the facilitator yells, "A-LAY!" and everyone spins around to face into the middle the circle, throwing their hands into the air when they yell the response, "A-LAY!"

The best way to do this activity is to give the directions and just jump in.

NOTES

Bamabale is a song that came to me in a dream many years ago.

The words to the chorus:

Bam-ba-lay, may bam-ba-lay
Bam-ba-lay, may jum-juh-wah
Bam-ba-lay, may bam-ba-lay
Bam-ba-lay, may jum-juh-wah
A-lay!

VARIATIONS

If the participants are skilled enough, encourage them to play more than just the Pulse as they step and rotate the circle. Remember, it does not have to be a complicated rhythm pattern, and you can use the CD as a guide. You can speed up the song and Pulse as the group gets more comfortable.

Sing and celebrate!

CD Track Six: Che Che Kule (chay=chay=coo=lay)

GROUP SIZE
Minimum: 4
Maximum: 40 +
Challenge Level: 1

TIME
5 minutes *(CD Track Length)*

INSTRUMENTS
This works well with just about any instrument (one per participant), or just clapping hands.
The facilitator should use an instrument (like a cowbell or jam block) that can be heard above the group.

FORMATION
Conglomerate *(facing the group with instruments...read on and see!)*

INSTRUCTIONS
1) Divide the large group into two smaller groups. In turn, one group will play, and the other will dance!

2) Choose the group that will play first. With your help, have them begin a groove that they can steadily hold (it does not have to be the same groove as on the CD; that's just for reference). It should be relatively simple, as they will eventually get going pretty fast (you might provide the Pulse if needed).

3) Once they have the groove, begin the dance with the other group. Do call and response (as it's done on the CD) and integrate the movements for each line of the song.

Here are the movements and words (spelled phonetically):

  a) **Chay Chay Coo-lay**
   Shake your head side to side (bending your head so your ears move towards your shoulders).

b) **Chay Ko-fee-sa**
   Hold your hands above head, quickly rolling palm over palm.

c) **Ko-fee-sa Lang-ga**
   Hold your arms outstretched to the sides, and shake or "shimmy" your shoulders.

d) **Lang-ga too Lang-ga**
   Place your hands on your hips, and wiggle your hips side to side.

e) **Aay-a-yeah-deh**
   Kick your feet out in front.

f) *Clap four times to the Pulse, then start again from the top!*

4) As demonstrated on the CD, increase the tempo with each round until you are all out of breath or the group playing instruments is going too fast to hold the groove. Then, switch so the other group can play percussion, and the musicians now dance.

NOTES

This is a song from Ghana, typically sung by children. On the CD, I have used the "Sinté" (Sin-tay) dun-dun rhythm along with a common djembe accompaniment rhythm. The rhythm you use can be any groove that's easy for your participants to play. Make sure the instrument players and dancers switch roles; it's important for each group to have the other experience.

VARIATIONS

This can be done with just clapping and singing; no instruments are needed.

Ready for the jam...

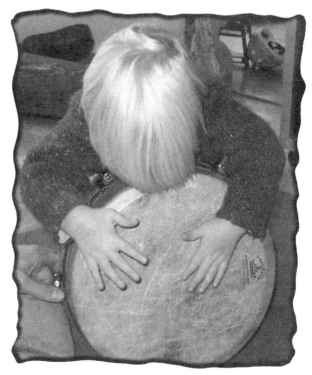

All that jammin' makes me ready for a nap!

Resources

"Happiness is not a matter of intensity but of balance, order, rhythm and harmony"

Thomas Merton

OVERVIEW

These days we are lucky to have an abundance of drumming and rhythm information available at our fingertips (Internet) and in our various communities. There are websites, books, CD's, videos, and teachers ready to share great info and keep the inspiration for drumming and rhythm alive and well. On the following pages you'll see some of my favorites, and this is by no means a complete list. Start your search at Google or your local music or bookstore and a whole world of information will open up for you. *NOTE: All Internet addresses were current as of publication date.*

Also, I've included a sampling of ideas to get your entire rhythm bag filled by visiting the hardware store. Depending on your skills with power tools, hardware stores have limitless possibilities. The ideas I have here are mostly "off the shelf and ready to play," with a couple of simple projects. If you have a super idea for a percussion instrument, I'd love to hear about it!

For more great ideas, visit:

www.rhythmweb.com/homemade/index.html

(FANTASTIC RESOURCE! These guys stay up late designing and testing homemade percussion.)

www.nancymusic.com/PRINThomemade.htm

www.childrensmuseum.org/artsworkshop/jam.html

www.mudcat.org/kids

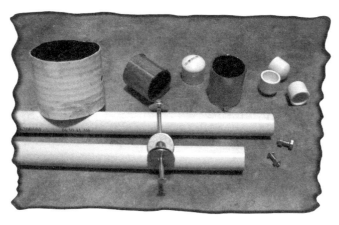

Raw materials...

Hardware Store Percussion Extravaganza!

For the budget conscious, never fear; you can outfit a full percussion ensemble with minimal cash outlay and supplies from your local hardware store.

Here are some ideas I've used with great success. Let me know if you find more hardware store surprises that work well for you.

DOWELS
Dowels make good alternatives to drumsticks. Choose a hardwood variety (oak is best), and no thinner than 3/8's of an inch for long lasting sticks. 12 to 14 inches make the best length. You may want to get a few thicker dowels (say ½ to ¾ of an inch) for thicker playing surfaces. To make large beaters, you can wrap the ends of thick dowels with old socks stuffed with foam or cloth, and hold that in place with good ol' duct tape. Keep in mind that anything wrapped or taped to dowels will, after some good hard play, fall off.

PLASTIC BUCKETS
The 5 gallon size utility buckets work best; they are durable and should cost no more than $5.00 a piece. With all buckets or bins, I recommend having players tilt them while playing. This way, the lower tones can resonate and adds a lot more to the sound. Also, hitting the sides and edges provide another tone for getting creative with grooves. Be careful not to use thick dowels on the buckets, as hard hitting with these will crack the plastic.

METAL BUCKETS
These are great for a different sound, but after a good round of pounding, they will dent and begin to loose their tonal quality. Using smaller sizes with smaller sticks or dowels will increase their longevity.

PLASTIC BUCKET LIDS
The heavy-duty versions make excellent surfaces for playing...like a low cost version of Sound Shapes®!

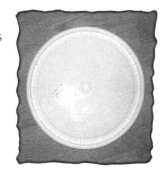

PLASTIC TRASH BINS

These range in size from the bathroom variety to huge 50-gallon monsters. All are great to have in an ensemble, but adjust the thickness of the sticks used so you don't break them on the first use. Go for the types with the most rigid plastic, as they have the best sound and durability. The deep bass of the large bins (30 to 50 gallon) are cool if you can get 4 or more in an ensemble.

METAL TRASHCAN LIDS

Some truly loud sounds! These are a winner in the volume department, so don't get too many or they'll be all you hear in your ensemble.

METAL PIPE BELLS

Get 2 to 3 inch diameter galvanized conduit and cut it into 4 to 8 inch lengths. Diameters larger than 3 inches are a bit large for hands to hold. **Danger:** Make sure to grind or sand down the sharp edges so folks don't cut their hands while they play! Use 4 to 6 inch bolts as beaters; you could hit the pipe pieces with dowels, but in vigorous, large ensemble playing, this will quickly splinter your dowels. I've used pipe pieces mounted to PVC handles and they work quite well (see the picture below).

EMPTY PAINT CAN SHAKERS

Small paint cans make great shakers when filled with a few small nuts (i.e., nuts and bolt kinds of nuts not peanuts). Make sure to tap the lids on well so they don't explode in a rigorous rhythm session.

PVC WHACK DRUMS

Use various lengths of 2 to 4 inch diameter PVC (schedule 40). Start with 2½ to 3 foot lengths, cap one end of the pipes, and use 4 x 6 inch squares of rubber matting (or flip-flops) to whack the open tops of the tubes. These won't be the loudest instruments in the collection, but they sure have a cool sound.

PVC DRAIN CAPS

4 inch PVC drain caps are compact and versatile to use. By striking them on the edge or center with a dowel or a drumstick, you can get a nice range of sounds and tones. And they are lound enugh to be played with a full circle of drums.

HARDWARE RATATAK SHAKERS

These are modern versions of the traditional *Ratatak* shaker from Ghana.

For the noise making discs of the shaker, you can use:

> The flat metal discs that are a part of canning jar lids;
> Metal lids from small paint cans; or,
> The platters from old hard drives (like I've done in the pictures...those babies are loud!).

Take 2 to 3 of those discs/lids and drill a hole in the center (hard drive platters already have a hole).

Sandwich the disks between fender washers and thread them all on a bolt. Attach the bolt to a thick dowel or 1-inch schedule 40 PVC (see the picture). Make sure the washers and discs can easily move up and down the bolt. Players will hold the lower part of the dowel or PVC, shake, rattle, and roll!

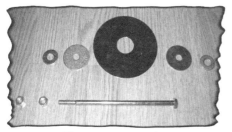

The necessary hardware

Arranging the hardware

The necessary PVC

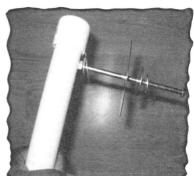

Completed shakers

PVC SHAKERS

Use two 2 inch PVC pipe caps and an 8 inch long section of 2 inch PVC pipe. Prime and glue one of the caps to the piece of pipe. Pour ¼ cup of steel in to the pipe. Prime and glue the other cap to the pipe; voila, a nice tube shaker! For the tube shakers I have pictured, I glued some colorful cloth around the pipe piece before gluing on the caps. These shakers store well, and are loud enough for drum circles, though their weight makes for a good arm workout!

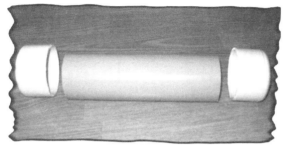

The PVC parts

The BB's

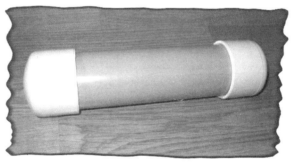

A completed shaker

A completed shaker wrapped in cloth

Rhythm Instrument Resources

If you are looking for the best places to get your eggs, sticks, Sound Shapes®, and the Boomwhackers® Tuned Percussion Tubes, here are some great places to look on line. Also, remember to check with your local music stores.

www.westmusic.com
One of the largest catalog distributors of the Boomwhackers® tubes, Sound Shapes®, and musical instruments. Their salespeople are knowledgeable and very friendly!

www.boomwhackers.com
The home of Whacky Music, Inc., and the birthplace of the Boomwhackers® Percussion Tubes.

www.shakerman.com
Wonderful site for all kinds of groovy instruments, and a great place for the Boomwhackers® Percussion Tubes. The owner, "Shakerman," is a great person to work with!

www.familymusicstore.com
American Music has knowledgeable salespeople and often offer great bulk pricing for schools.

www.johnsmusic.com
An excellent store in Seattle, and a *fantastic* selection of instruments and books on line!

www.music123.com
These folks have a large selection and pretty good prices.

www.musiciansfriend.com
One of the best places to get inexpensive drumsticks *(Promotional Hickory Drumsticks, Product #444616).* Also great for egg shakers when they are on sale *(Product #441640).*

Drumming: Musical Resources

This list of recordings offers a small sample of the wonderful world of drumming. They are great places to start your exploration of drum and percussion based music.

ARTIST	TITLE	STYLE
Mamady Keita *(Master drummer)*	*All titles* *(Wassolon, Afo, etc.)*	Traditional West African
Famoudou Konaté *(Master drummer)*	*All titles*	Traditional West African
Babatunde Olatunji *(Master drummer)*	*Drums of Passion* *(And all other titles)*	Traditional West African
Professor Trance *(Contemporary grooves)*	*Shaman's Breath,* *Medicine Drum*	Trance Dance
Mickey Hart *(Traditional with modern)*	*Planet Drum,* *(And all other titles)*	Great mix of grooves!
Gabriel Roth *(Traditional with modern)*	*All albums* *(She has at least 10)*	Trance Dance
Fara Tolno *(Master drummer)*	*Binye*	Traditional West African
Glen Velez *(Master drummer)*	*All titles*	Masterful Frame Drums
Geoff Johns	*Drum!*	Great Educational CD
Kenya Masala	*Juju! Volume I* *(Great for classroom)*	Folk West African

Drumming: Written Resources

There are so many wonderful books on drumming, listing them would require an entire book. I've chosen some my favorites as suggested starters for your personal library.

AUTHOR	TITLE
Arthur Hull	*Drum Circle Spirit* THF Drum circle facilitation book Includes a CD
Christine Stevens	*The Art and Heart of Drum Circles* Another great book on drum circle facilitation
Martin Klabunde	*West African Rhythms Sourcebook* Excellent culture and rhythm information Includes notations and a CD
Mamady Keita	*My Life for the Djembe* Amazing culture and rhythm information Includes notations and a CD
Bill Matthews	*Drum Talk (also Conga Joy)* Great rhythm notations and info; Available as a CD or video in VHS format
Christine Stevens Lynn Kliener	*Sound Shape Playbook* More great Sound Shape® games by two masterful facilitators; with CD
Layne Redmond	*When the Drummers Were Women -* *A Spiritual History of Rhythm* Fascinating history and lore
Kalani	*All About Jembe* *All About Bongo (and Conga)* Wonderful educational and "learn to play" books; Kalani also has educational videos and CD's

AUTHOR	TITLE

Yaya Diallo   *The Healing Drum*
Drum history and lore from a West African Master

Sule Greg Wilson   *The Drummer's Path*
Spirituality and energy of drumming from a very
knowledgable drumming historian

Robert Lawrence Friedman
The Healing Power of the Drum
Amazing stories that demonstrate the power rhythm
and drumming have for healing

Mickey Hart   *Planet Drum / Drumming at the Edge*
In depth drum history and lore from a master of many
percussion instruments and the former drummer of
The Grateful Dead

Rocky Maffit   *Rhythm and Beauty*
Well done overview of global percussion instruments
with wonderful pictures; includes a CD

Drumming: Web Sites

There are so many amazing websites devoted to drumming and drum circle facilitation, I'd have to devote a whole book to do them all justice. The following short list is a wonderful place to get started. Be sure to see the "links" page at each site...massive amounts of resources!

www.rhythmoflifedrumming.com / www.sourceconsultinggroup.com
Kenya's sites, great resources, and wonderful programs!

www.remo.com
Excellent drums, fantastic resources...be sure to check out the Health Rhythms section!

www.ttmusa.org
Mamady Keita is the West African master (Djembefola) of the djembe drum.

www.ubdrumcircles.com
Fantastic drumming programs, great books, and must read articles.

www.rhythmconnection.net
The source for Drum and Dance info in Austin, Texas

www.drumcircle.com
Arthur Hull is the "Granddaddy" of Community Drumming.

www.dambe.org
An organization providing wonderful educational programs.

www.handsondrum.com
Jim Greiner is a fantastic drum circle facilitator, with excellent corporate programs!

www.drumcafe.com
Incredible international corporate drumming experiences; tons of fun!

www.azrhythmconnection.com
Frank Thompson (REMO endorsed facilitator), an energizing Rhythm Facilitator and team-building specialist

www.kalanimusic.com
A wonderful drum circle facilitator and drum teacher with great books, videos and CD resources

www.johnsmusic.com
Books (huge selection), videos, CD's, instruments; they've got it all

www.rhythmtraders.com
Excellent resource for CD's, books, and instruments.

www.mhart.com/Pages/senspeech.html
*A powerful speech by **Grateful Dead** drummer Mickey Hart on the Health benefits of drumming.*

www.drums.org
Connections to the drum and dance classes in the U.S. and the world!

www.djembe.org
Organized links to drum and dance information around the country.

www.drumjourney.com
An excellent resource listing drum teachers and drum circle facilitators, as well as info on drums and rhythm.

www.drumzaustin.com
A wonderful place to get beautiful traditional drums.

www.drumskulls.com
Another place for beautiful traditional drums.

www.swps.org
The Seattle World Percussion Society is the sponsor of the annual World Rhythm Festival in Seattle.

Resources for Children's Music:

www.musicrhapsody.com
Lynn Kleiner is one of the best facilitators and writers of children's rhythm activities.

www.childrensmusic.org
The Children's Music Web is a wonderful and comprehensive resource.

www.cmnonline.org
The Children's Music Network: Folks across the country who care about quality children's music.

www.childrensmusicworkshop.com
Lots of great info on children's music programming.

www.younghrt.com
Youngheart Music; great products and information.

Rhythm Recipe Ideas (4-count)

As you use these syllables for rhythm, let them swing! That is, play with the feel of the syllables and the natural sing-song way they can flow from the tongue. Recipes can include words taken from your group's specific focus; for example, team-buil-ding, or, inn-o-va-shun (innovation). One can use a mission statement or a set of guidelines...you name it. For the classroom, rhythm with vocabulary words history facts, or math skills makes the learning process fun and dependable (just think of how popular rap music has become!).

The following are basic ideas to get you started; the possibilities are infinite!

PIZZA IDEAS

Deep-dish-peet-za (pizza)
Lots-a-moz-a-rell-a
Cut-up-some-mush-rooms
Love-that-pepp-er-o-ni
How-bout-some-on-yons (onions)
Green-pep-per-makes-it-great

SMOOTHIE IDEAS

3-or-4-ba-na-nas
Blue-be-rry-ice-cream
Add-some-a-pple-juice
Pee-ches-and-cream
Throw-in-a-few-aw-monds
Scops-of-ice-cream-mmm-mmm-mmm

COOKIE IDEAS

Oat-meal-ra-sins
Chok-late-chunks
Add-some-eggs-to-make-em-flu-fie (fluffy)
Swee-ten-them-with-lots-of-shu-gar (sugar)
Mix-in-the-butt-er
Eat-them-up-with-milk

VEGGIE SALAD IDEAS

Start-with-lots-a-let-tice (lettuce)
Cut-to-ma-toes-slice-by-slice
Cu-cum-ber-weh-jes (wedges)-make-ev-ry (every)-thing-nice
Some-folks-like-greens-and-gar-lic
Ra-dish-es-spice-the-mix-just-right
Oil-an-vin-a-gar-splash-it-on

FRUIT SALAD IDEAS

Wash-up-some-grapes-and-put-them-in
Or-ran-ges-and-a-pples
Cree-me-ba-na-nas-make-it-all-taste-good
Top-it-all-off-with-ca-shew-nuts
Sprin-kle-a-dash-of-cin-a-mon

STEW SONG

Down-in-loo-see-anna-wher-da-gum-bow's-hot
A-touch-a-dis-a-touch-a-dat-that's-a-lot!
A-bit-o-chilli-pepp-er / to-mek-da-tounge-sing
Den-toss-in-a-po-ta-toe-ring-a-ding-ding
Now-we-scoop-it-o-vah-rice
An-we-eat-it-up-real-nice
Wash-it-down-wit-extra-gra-vee
Pat-mah-belly-feelin-lazee!

RHYTHM SONG

My-big-drum-goes-boom-boom-boom
It-shakes-tha-house-it-shakes-tha-room
I-play-the-met-al-bell / go-in'-clang-clang-clang
It's-so-much-low-der / than-when-I-sang
We-rock-on-the-pulse / coun-tin'-2-3-4
The-groo-vee-fat-beats-make-you-want-lots-more
So-don't-be-shy-you-can-make-some-noise
Playin'-rid-ims-good-fa-girls / an-its-al-so-good-fa-boys

Activity Skills Index

"There's a whole lot of rhythm going round..."
Parliament

OVERVIEW

The activities in this book are multifaceted, and can be used to facilitate learning on many levels beyond increased rhythmic ability. This sections outlines the primary skills practiced or developed by an activity. Keep in mind that the learning experience is dependent on *your* intentions for the activity; the way you facilitate the process directly affects the outcome. This index is primarily an overview and you may find more specific skill building occurring as you become comfortable with the various activities.

Along the with skill focus, the index reviews the challenge level for each activity (ranging from 0 to 5). A challenge level of "0" means the activity is very easy to facilitate and easy for participants to do with little explanation. These are great energizers, warm up or quick transition activities. A challenge level of "5" means there is more facilitation required, and more skill building happening during the activity. These are great for problem solving and focused team building and you may want to debrief the experience to support learning. Regardless of the challenge level, each activity can be modified to make it easier or more difficult depending on your group.

The index also provides information on the best age group for each activity. The age groups are general:
Youngers: K to 3rd grade
Middles: 4th to 6th grade
Olders: 7th to 10th grade
Adults: 10th grade to Adults
Use this as a guide and remember that simple modifications to an activity make it easier or harder depending on the makeup of your group.

Even though these activities can be used to teach and to learn, their primary intent remains simple: have fun!

Brain Rhythm (Pg. 18)

Specific Skill Focus: Kinesthetic (body) awareness, Listening, Multi-tracking, Focusing

Best Age Group: Can be modified to work with all age groups

Challenge Level: 0

The Pulse (Pg. 20)

Specific Skill Focus: Listening, Cooperation, Group Cohesion and Connection, Concentration and Focus

Best Age Group: Can be modified to work with all age groups

Challenge Level: 0

Rhythm in the Kitchen (Pg. 22)

Specific Skill Focus: Listening, Cooperation, Creativity

Best Age Group: Can be modified to work with all age groups

Challenge Level: 1

Shake the Eggs   (Pg. 27)

Specific Skill Focus: Listening, Following directions, Group Cohesion

Best Age Group: Can be modified to work with all age groups

Challenge Level: 1

Eggs Up Eggs Down Down   (Pg. 29)

Specific Skill Focus: Listening, Following Directions, Concentration and Focus

Best Age Group: Can be modified to work with all age groups

Challenge Level: 0

Eggstremely Quiet   (Pg. 31)

Specific Skill Focus: Listening, Concentration and Focus, Integrity

Best Age Group: Middles through Adults

Challenge Level: 2

Amoebeggs   (Pg. 33)

Specific Skill Focus: Cooperation, Creativity, Problem Solving, Group Cohesion

Best Age Group: Middles through Adults

Challenge Level: 2

Take It Pass It   (Pg. 34)

Specific Skill Focus: Listening, Cooperation, Group Cohesion and Connection

Best Age Group: Middles through Adults

Challenge Level: 2

Egg Drop Soup   (Pg. 38)

Specific Skill Focus: Cooperation, Creativity, Problem Solving, Concentration and Focus

Best Age Group: Olders through Adults

Challenge Level: 3

Call and Response   (Pg. 43)

Specific Skill Focus: Listening, Cooperation, Concentration and Focus, Group Cohesion

Best Age Group: Can be modified to work with all age groups

Challenge Level: 0

World Tour   (Pg. 45)

Specific Skill Focus: Cooperation, Group Cohesion

Best Age Group: Can be modified to work with all age groups

Challenge Level: 0

Stick-Stick-Shoe-Floor   (Pg. 47)

Specific Skill Focus: Listening, Cooperation, Concentration and Focus, Group Cohesion

Best Age Group: Can be modified to work with all age groups

Challenge Level: 1

Sound of One   (Pg. 49)

Specific Skill Focus: Listening, Cooperation, Problem Solving, Creativity, Communication

Best Age Group: Middles through Adults

Challenge Level: 3

Sticky Situation   (Pg. 51)

Specific Skill Focus: Listening, Problem Solving, Concentration and Focus

Best Age Group: Middles through Adults

Challenge Level: 2

My Sticks Your Sticks (Pg. 53)

Specific Skill Focus: Listening, Cooperation, Group Cohesion, Problem Solving, Communication

Best Age Group: Olders through Adults

Challenge Level: 3

My Sticks Your Sticks Dosie Do (Pg. 58)

Specific Skill Focus: Listening, Cooperation, Group Cohesion, Problem Solving, Communication

Best Age Group: Olders through Adults

Challenge Level: 4

My Sticks Your Sticks Challenge (Pg. 61)

Specific Skill Focus: Listening, Cooperation, Group Cohesion, Problem Solving, Communication

Best Age Group: Olders through Adults

Challenge Level: 5

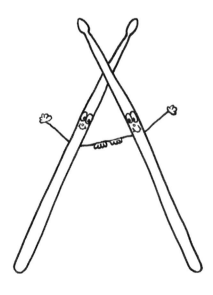

Play a Boom Together (Pg. 65)

Specific Skill Focus: Listening, Cooperation, Group Cohesion, Communication

Best Age Group: Can be modified to work with all age groups

Challenge Level: 0

Peek a Boom (Pg. 67)

Specific Skill Focus: Listening, Group Cohesion, Concentration and Focus

Best Age Group: Can be modified to work with all age groups

Challenge Level: 1

1 Boom, 2 Boom, Red Boom, Blue Boom (Pg. 69)

Specific Skill Focus: Listening, Cooperation, Group Cohesion, Concentration and Focus

Best Age Group: Can be modified to work with all age groups

Challenge Level: 2

Colors of the Rhythm (Pg. 71)

Specific Skill Focus: Listening, Cooperation, Group Cohesion, Creativity, Concentration and Focus

Best Age Group: Middles through Adults

Challenge Level: 3

Maculele (Pg. 73)

Specific Skill Focus: Cooperation, Creativity, Concentration and Focus, Problem Solving, Communication

Best Age Group: Olders through Adults

Challenge Level: 5

Math Pulse (Pg. 79)

Specific Skill Focus: Listening, Cooperation, Group Cohesion, Concentration and Focus, Basic Math Skills

Best Age Group: Can be modified to work with all age groups

Challenge Level: 1

Shape Up! (Pg. 81)

Specific Skill Focus: Listening, Cooperation, Problem Solving, Creativity

Best Age Group: Can be modified to work with all age groups

Challenge Level: 1

Size Em' Up (Pg. 83)

Specific Skill Focus: Listening, Cooperation, Group Cohesion, Concentration and Focus

Best Age Group: Middles through Adults

Challenge Level: 1

Soup's on (Pg. 85)

Specific Skill Focus: Listening, Cooperation, Group Cohesion, Creativity

Best Age Group: Middles to Adults

Challenge Level: 2

Bowl a' Beats (Pg. 87)

Specific Skill Focus: Listening, Cooperation, Problem Solving, Communication

Best Age Group: Olders through Adults

Challenge Level: 4

Beat Vortex   (Pg. 89)

Specific Skill Focus: Listening, Cooperation, Problem Solving, Communication

Best Age Group: Olders through Adults

Challenge Level: 5

Top Ten Challenge   (Pg. 91)

Specific Skill Focus: Listening, Cooperation, Problem Solving, Communication, Creativity

Best Age Group: Olders through Adults

Challenge Level: 5

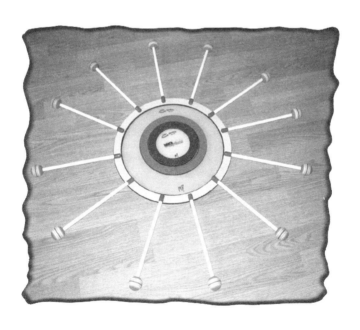

Rhythm Machine (Pg. 95)

Specific Skill Focus: Listening, Cooperation, Group Cohesion,

Best Age Group: Can be modified to work with all age groups

Challenge Level: 1

Small Group Groove (Pg. 97)

Specific Skill Focus: Listening, Cooperation, Group Cohesion, Creativity

Best Age Group: Middles through Adults

Challenge Level: 2

Rhythm Stories (Pg. 99)

Specific Skill Focus: Listening, Cooperation, Group Cohesion, Creativity, Language Arts

Best Age Group: Middles through Adults

Challenge Level: 2

Rhythm Conversations (Pg. 101)

Specific Skill Focus: Listening, Cooperation, Group Cohesion, Creativity, Language Arts

Best Age Group: Olders through Adults

Challenge Level: 3

Sound Wave (Pg. 103)

Specific Skill Focus: Listening, Cooperation, Group Cohesion, Concentration and Focus, Problem Solving

Best Age Group: Olders through Adults

Challenge Level: 3

Follow the Leader   (Pg. 105)

Specific Skill Focus: Listening, Cooperation, Group Cohesion, Creativity

Best Age Group: Olders through Adults

Challenge Level: 4

If I Play...   (Pg. 107)

Specific Skill Focus: Listening, Cooperation, Group Cohesion, Concentration and Focus, Problem Solving, Math Skills

Best Age Group: Olders through Adults

Challenge Level: 4

About the Author...

Kenya S. Masala is a charismatic community and human development consultant, certified teacher and curriculum specialist. His unique blend of skills as an educator, facilitator, and percussionist inspire real learning and community building with clients ranging from the corporate world to youth. He provides interactive keynotes, facilitates seminars, leadership and youth development training, ropes courses, and educational percussion programs. He also designs and develops multimedia curricula and presentations on a national level.

Kenya enthusiastically creates highly effective learning and community building experiences, authentically motivating individuals and groups of all ages.

Kenya is a REMO Drums endorsed drumming facilitator.

For more information, and to schedule trainings or order materilas, contact Kenya at:
www.sourceconsultinggroup.com
www.rhythmoflifedrumming.com
kenya@sourceconsultinggroup.com